THE
PASTOR'S
wife

THE LIFE AND ROLE OF THE PASTOR'S WIFE

BY PEGGY AMA DONKOR

THE PASTOR'S WIFE
The Life and Role of The Pastor's Wife

Contact
Peggy Ama Donkor
+233 (0) 244 269 352
Peggyamadonkor@gmail.com
GBC, 2nd Kanda Link
GA 005-8607

ISBN 978 – 9988 – 3 – 7451 – 8

All scriptures are from the NIV unless otherwise stated.

Layout and Cover Design by
Sarah Broni
+233 (0) 208 509 679
mssarahbroni@gmail.com

Printed by
Ultimate Solution Publications
Kumasi
+233 (0) 244 884 327

DEDICATION

This book is dedicated to the loving memory of the late Osofomaame, Hannah Osei-Korsah, nee Hammond, who went to be with the Lord at age 48 in 2022 after a brief complaint of heartache.

ACKNOWLEDGEMENT

To the ever-merciful God, who is no respecter of persons, to him be all the glory and honor for placing on my heart this project in memory of a dear friend turned sister- Hannah Ama Nyamaah (Mrs. Osei-Korsah).

Next in line and worth appreciating is Apostle Dr. Philip Osei-Korsah, husband of Ama Nyamaah who willingly and carefully thought through before allowing me even use her picture for the cover of this book. Thank you, Papa, for showing Ama true love in the sense of the word.

To the fourth Chairman of The Church of Pentecost, Apostle Dr. Michael Kwabena Ntumy, who before passing on to glory, gladly wrote the forward of the book, and added that, "A book from you is long overdue."

To the Director of the Pentecost Men's Ministry, Apostle Vincent Anane Denteh, who readily and gladly recommended, Elder VCT Ofinam-Antwi, Chief Editor, of the Pentecost Press Ltd, who in spite of his tight schedule on the job, agreed to help prepare the manuscript for the printers. Special appreciation to Elder Fred Tettey Amoako, Deputy Editor at the Media Ministry of The Church of Pentecost Headquarters, for doing the final proof reading.

Worthy of mention is Mrs. Gifty Dansoah Appiah, who made time to fine tune the project. I am equally indebted to all pastors' wives, both home and abroad, known and unknown, who freely shared experiences from their ministerial journey with me. But for you, this work would have been but a dream.

How can I forget the four national service ladies – Deborah, Gloria, Hindatu, and Racheal who had to sometimes hold the fort for me while I worked on the manuscript. May Jehovah overdo it for you.

Now, to the movers and shakers of God's kingdom on earth, church leaders, my prayer is that these golden nuggets shared by our church mothers would influence policy in one way or the other for the necessary consideration and implementation, to make them more effective as they labor in God's vineyard alongside our pastors.

Finally, to you, reading this book, my prayer is that, as you read the views of these church mothers you will have an insight into their lives, and if you ever thought being a pastor's wife is a walk in the park, you would revise your notes and also remember to bear them up in prayers for maximum impact for the church public and beyond.

CONTENT

ENDORSEMENTS

"The Pastor's Wife - the role and life of the Pastor's wife" is a well written, insightful real-life Ode to Pastor's wives. The author, a renowned broadcast journalist, writing in a simple, relatable English, gives the reader a peek into the pastor's wife's (Osofo/Asafo maame's) lonely and often misunderstood unscripted life.

She translates her pain from the loss of a dear friend into an opportunity to give pastors' wives a voice to share her secret pain and burdens to the world, not in a sense of drawing sympathy but in an appreciation of their public life, which has virtually overshadowed their individuality and a "living above reproach." She reveals how some pastors' wives have virtually lost themselves in ministry as they submissively help their spouses work towards fulfilling the mandate of their calling.

This is a must-read for all church members to help them to appreciate the vulnerability and secret cries of the pastor's spouse. It does not paint a gloomy picture, but rather sheds light on the reality and how the situation can be made better through policies that allow the wives to also live their calling as they support the Pastor.

Deaconess Sophia Nana Kudjordi, Pentecost International Worship Centre (PIWC), Graceland, Chief Corporate Communications Officer, ZoomLion.

In the book, Peggy has raised questions about the preparations that ministers' wives are taken through and how this affects them in their roles. She does this by picking on the perceptives of a cross-section of ministers' wives drawn from a number of denominations in Ghana and beyond. The author does all these by beautifully weaving the biography of a minister's wife and how she viewed her life from up-close.

Based on these, she considered the challenges faced by ministers' wives and offers some useful recommendations to improve the ministry of ministers' wives.

The book has a great deal of credibility and specificity. I am hopeful that it will galvanize ministers and wives in appreciating the circumstances within which ministry is done and I will recommend it for all.

Samuel Gyau Obuobi (Apostle) General Secretary, The Church of Pentecost

Having begun as a dirge in honor of her late childhood friend, Mrs. Hannah Osei-Korsah, the writer, Peggy Ama Donkor, has turned her tribute into a very inspiring discourse about the architecture of the ministry of pastors' wives.

This book is infused with various perspectives and vital information for ministers of the gospel and their wives and by extension, church leadership.

Vincent Anane Denteh (Apostle) Director, Pentecost Men's Ministry, Executive Council Member, CoP, National Coordinator, Pentecost Chieftaincy Ministry.

It is interesting how Peggy Ama Donkor chooses to delve into the rare subject of the role ministers' wives play in the life of ministers in the body of Christ.

In her book, "The Pastor's wife-The life and role of the Pastor's wife', she recounts the life story of her late "sister" as a minister's wife and weaves that into the role of other ministers' wives from The Church of Pentecost and other Christian denominations.

The author raises questions about the role ministers' wives play in the ministry of their husbands. She places in context the role of the minister's wife in The Church of Pentecost by drawing parallels with that of other churches. Having obtained the views of a wide array of ministers' wives, she then enumerates a number of challenges faced by the ministers' wives across the spectrum, offer recommendations in addressing some of those challenges as suggested by those already in ministry. She also has a word for wives of young ministers and those of new ministerial entrants.

Undoubtedly, the author has made use of her journalistic expertise to spice up the writings. The result is this very simple and easy to read book, and one appropriate for all categories of persons. I will encourage everyone to obtain copies, and your perception of who a minister's wife is, will be changed for good.

Elder Engr. Eric Atta-Sonno, Head, Project Development and Operations Department, Ghana Libyan-Arab Holding Company, Pentecost International Worship Centre, PIWC Atomic.

As a minister's wife, mother and career/professional woman, I understand the unique challenges and blessings that come with this role, and I can confidently say that this book. "THE PASTOR'S WIFE: The Role and Life of the Pastor's Wife" is an individual resource for anyone in a similar position or seeking, a better understanding, of the life of a pastor's wife in our contemporary world.

Peggy Ama Donkor has managed to not only shed light on the frequently overloaded and misunderstood role of a pastor's wife, but also provides insightful direction, encouragement and wisdom. This book covers everything from handling congregational expectations to managing, the delicate balance of family, ministry and career.

She draws from her own experiences as well as the experiences of other pastors' wives to provide genuine, relatable stories that resonate with the reader's heart, providing comfort and assurance to those who may feel isolated in their role.

Throughout the pages of this book, you will discover practical advice on managing time, nurturing relationships and expectations, while maintaining a strong faith and deep connection with God. It is both a guidebook and a source of comfort and inspiration.

In my opinion, THE PASTOR'S WIFE: The Role and Life of the Pastor's Wife "is a must read for every pastor's wife who is just starting out or have been on this path for years. It is also a great resource for pastors, church leaders and anyone who wants to better understand and support the ministry of pastors' wives.

Mrs. Gifty Dansoah Appiah- Strategy, Development Planning and Management Expert.

FOREWARD

This is a soft and tenderly written book by a woman about a special woman in the church called the Pastor's Wife (P.W), who she is, and her role. The solemn fact is that the author is neither a theologian nor a Pastor's Wife. She is a serial award-winning broadcast journalist with Ghana Broadcasting Corporation's GBC (GTV), the national television channel. Sister Peggy Ama Donkor, the author, whom I fondly call Auntie Ama, has won 12 awards related to her field and the prestigious Journalist of the Year (2005) award by the Ghana Journalists Association (G.J.A.), the ultimate journalistic award in the country.

Using her avid journalistic skills and those derived from her nearly 40 years of discipleship training and as a Sunday School Teacher in The Church of Pentecost, she was able to glean from the Bible the role of a Pastor's Wife, basing mostly on 1 Timothy 3:11 and also from character studies of some leading women of the Pauline era.

The author does not come from a know-it-all perspective to prescribe a job description for pastors' wives. Job descriptions, roles and functions, are issued by organizations to their employees. In the case of churches, like The Church of Pentecost, they are issued to pastors, not their spouses. It is the former who are licensed to minister, not the latter. Consequently, the pastor's wife, by virtue of being married to a pastor, is called upon to perform a role which is unscripted, nondescript, and can be as amorphous as it is unsettling. The author therefore resorts to extensive use of the scanty literature available. Besides, she garners vital nuggets from senior church ministers whom she dubs "fathers." To crown it all, sister Peggy Ama Donkor embarks upon an impressive triangular, continental interview of thirty-five ministers' wives in Africa, Europe and North America. Here, some of the respondents went beyond narrating their roles as pastors' wives to opening up and sharing their challenges, frustrations, pains, but nevertheless, their non-regrets of being pastors' wives.

The author catalogues these challenges and calls upon various stakeholders to introduce policies and implement initiatives to improve the lot of ministers' wives.

Auntie Ama is not a pastor's wife, so how competent and knowledgeable of issues affecting them is she, to be able to write such a book? In answering this, we may ask another question: "Should one necessarily have been a professional, participant or practitioner to be competent enough to coach others?" My research landed me on Muhammad Ali, nee Cassius Clay of USA. He is the celebrated heavyweight boxer of all time and the BBC Sportsman of the 20th Century. In his 21-years fighting career (1960-1981), he won 56 of these 61 fights and is the only man in history to win the world heavyweight title three times. Amazingly, the coach of this "Greatest boxer of all times," Angelo Dundee, never fought in the ring. Dundee went on to train 15 people who became world boxing champions.

In the same way, some of Auntie Ama's Sunday school pupils are now Asafomaame and pastors serving in the church both home and abroad. She has created a social media platform-WhatsApp for them as a way of staying in touch. She also, had a bosom friend, a friend of over thirty short years, twenty of which, she was a pastor's wife, Mrs. Hannah Osei- Korsah. They grew up together, fellowshipped in the same local church, taught as Sunday school teachers and shared their thoughts, dreams and aspirations. When Hannah and husband were called into the full time- pastoral ministry, Peggy took keen interest in their ministry, monitored and visited them in their second station Tamale in northern Ghana and observed how the couple went about their ministry life.

Through these, Peggy got first -hand knowledge of the character and personality of the ideal pastor's wife and the role she is called upon to play. She did not only get to know what they do, or should be doing, but also experienced the challenges they encounter. Sister Peggy Ama Donkor would not have published such a book at this time but for a tragedy which occurred. Her bosom friend, Mrs. Hannah Osei-Korsah, died suddenly after a very busy weekend of church activities. This book is to eulogize and immortalize Hannah. Peggy's best tribute to her is to hold her up as the Ideal Pastor's Wife.

I recommend this book to:

Every Pastor's Wife: that they will be encouraged and never give up.

Every Pastor: that they will support their wives as they support them.

Every Presbytery member: that they will cherish their pastor's wife.

Every Church member: that they would love and support their pastor's wife.

Church Policy maker: that, where applicable, they would streamline the roles and responsibilities of pastors' wives.

Apostle Dr. Michael Ntumy

Order of The Volta, Companion

Chairman, The Church of Pentecost (1998-2008)

President, Ghana Pentecostal and Charismatic Council (1998-2008)

Chancellor, Pentecost University (2003-2008)

INTRODUCTION

Born and bred in the Catholic Church, growing up as a young Catholic, my desire was to become a NUN, or a Roman Sister as we call them. This idea excited not just me, but also my late mother, Mrs. Comfort Akosua Kumah Donkor, nee Donkor. I took everything about the church and its practices seriously. I got excited any time I saw these nuns going about their lives in their most, proper manner. Their impeccable white habits, scarf and rosary fascinated me. As a curious young person, I attended any Christian gathering meant for the youth in any community I found myself, irrespective of the denomination. As a result, I also got involved with other Christian denominations before joining The Church of Pentecost. While in Senior Secondary School, that is in Damongo Secondary School then in the Northern Region, now in the Savanna Region of Ghana, I played a key role in the Catholic Church and would normally take up either the first or second reading during Mass. I was also a member of the school's Scripture Union (SU) and later became the Prayer Secretary of the group.

I purposed in my heart not to defile myself, and akin to Daniel, I stayed away from what was considered the norm in most secondary schools in those days- the boyfriend-girlfriend relationships. Graciously, I became friends with my one-year senior, Livesy Abokyi, then commonly referred to as sister Livesy, now Dr. Mrs. Livesy Naafo Abokyi, we nicked named ourselves **HOSTA** in other words HOLY SISTERS- as we pledged to lead holy lives to please the Lord. Even now, at our advanced age, whenever the opportunity presents itself and we meet or speak on phone, we still call ourselves HOSTA. As a Catholic and SU member in school, I noticed, something which later led me to join The Church of Pentecost. It was a tradition or custom, for Form Five students, that is final-year students who were about writing their General Certificate of Education Ordinary Level (GCE 'O' Level) Examinations, to fellowship with The Church of Pentecost in Damongo town to be prayed for.

We as junior students and SU members followed them for such prayer sessions. Surprisingly, they did not just go to be prayed for, but also took part in every activity of the service- especially the Bible studies, and asked questions for clarification, something that was alien in the Catholic Church in those days. At a point, I had no choice but to inform the then Assistant Headmaster who was also a member of the Catholic Church on campus, of my desire to leave the Catholic Church. His response, was, "I knew you would leave one day, because you love to sing." But for me it was not about the songs, but rather the opportunity to read, digest and even ask questions during Bible studies. That, for me was great, since there were so many things I personally did not understand. That, for me, was the deciding factor. And today, here I am in The Church of Pentecost, where I have been fellowshipping for the past four decades and counting. Exiting the Catholic church meant that my desire to become a nun had been aborted, since The Church of Pentecost affirms the institution of marriage as sanctioned by God.

Growing up in The Church of Pentecost at Burma Camp, now the Garrison Church of Pentecost, we set out as six friends, Fidelia, Peggy, Agnes, Hannah, Anet, and the late Hannah, then Hannah Hammond. Among us, we knew that Fidelia and Hannah were cut for the calling of Osofomaame. Why because everything about them depicted such a lifestyle. It was therefore not surprising that in the year 2000, Hannah though the youngest was the first among us to marry, and to no other person than, then Elder Philip Osei-Korsah. "Hierarchically" in the church, aside the Pastor, the Pastor's Wife commonly referred to as *Osofomaame* in The Church of Pentecost, which loosely translates as the pastor's wife, is seen as the next in command. Osofomaame is a combination, of two Twi words- Osofo- PASTOR and Maame- MOTHER. Realistically, should we go by the

Akan (Twi) as its used, then the pastor's wife who is the mother of a congregation would rather be known as Asafomaame-congregation mother or mother of the congregation. The Pastor's Wife can be described as the first lady of the church or the lead woman in every congregation in The Church of Pentecost by some unwritten code- who works hand in hand with her husband to fulfil kingdom business. As six young ladies, two - Fidelia and Hannah, trained as professional teachers and married Pastors just a couple of years into marriage and became Asofomaame. The two, Mrs. Fidelia Blankson Akua Nyarko Sefa Sarfo and the late Hannah Ama Osei-Korsah, who died at a relatively young age of 48 in 2022, became ministry partners with their husbands. Why would she be the first to marry and the first to die? Could it be destiny or there is more to it? Getting over her death has not been easy. I am even wondering if I can ever get over it, because every year, I had the singular honor to make a birthday dedication for her on Radio/ Television.

It is this pain, that has led to the writing of this book you are holding in your hand. Why would such a lady who loved God die at her prime age? I keep wondering if combining her work as a professional teacher and later a Headmistress and Pastor's Wife weighed her down. Of course, others might have died at a much younger age, but the death of Osofomaame Hannah Osei -Korsah, who

I simply called AMA or HH - Hannah Hammond her maiden name, has affected me terribly. I have since then asked God so many WHYs to no avail, for His Word tells us that "all hidden things belong to the Lord" - Deuteronomy 29:29 - one of Hannah's favorite Bible quotations. I am by this volume, trying to find out exactly who a pastor's wife is, what her role (s) in ministry involves, what the low and high points of ministry are and what other golden nuggets I could garner for future generations.

In writing this book, my curiosity went beyond pastors' wives in The Church of Pentecost, the church, I belong to and where the late Osofomaame Hannah worshipped before her untimely demise, to include others from other denominations such as the Assemblies of God Ghana, The Apostolic Church Ghana, and the Presbyterian Church of Ghana. Other contributions equally came from Africa, the United Kingdom and United States of America. To delve into the details of who a pastor's wife is, we first, need to know who, Mrs. Hannah Osei-Korsah was.

Two

HANNAH OSEI-KORSAH

The late Mrs. Hannah Osei-Korsah, nee Hannah Ama Nyamaa Hammond, was born at Accra New Town, a suburb of Ghana's capital on Saturday, May 4, 1974, to the late Mr. Kwasi Gyan Hammond and the late Mrs. Juliana Agyei Hammond. Same year, her father got recruited into the Ghana Armed Forces- GAF. Two years on, that is in October 1976, the family moved to the Arakan Barracks, Burma Camp also in Accra. "Due to this, she was considered as a bearer of good fortune by her father. She was the last born among her five siblings and the only" left-handed among the siblings." Pastor Emmanuel Asamoah Gyan.

Hannah Ama Nyamah's first taste of education was at the 5th Battalion Primary and Junior High Schools at Burma Camp after which she gained admission into Labone Secondary School for her secondary education in 1992. As a military barrack girl, Hannah was a hard-working lady who helped her mother not just with house chores, but also in petty trading. She was not the type who engaged in unnecessary or unproductive friendship. She was a serious lady from scratch.

At The Church of Pentecost Burma Camp Assembly, where she worshipped, she was among the early birds to church. She was simply neat, and modest in her dressing. She wore slit and kaba, one of the traditional Ghanaian women's attires to the admiration of most of us. She would dance during praises beautifully and we as friends often teased, she danced like an Osofomaame and so was practicing her future role. She partook in every church activity and was very prayerful and was part of the "Amangoase" (under the mango tree) prayer team. During the leadership of Pastor Peter and Mama Esther Ayerakwa. She was a Prayer Warrior, and her prayer life went beyond amangoase, she would once in a while go to the football park with sister Happy Teye or Fidelia Nyarko to pray. Ama loved to sing, she knew almost all the Pentecostal tunes, in fact all the old songs. As to how she did it was a mystery to me. Anytime, I was not sure of the lyrics of any of the church songs, Ama was the go-to person. A classical one is, Pentecoste Asɔre Nnwom 148 below:

"Dwen papa a ɔye ma wo n"ho

Dwen papa a ɔye ma wo n"ho

Se ehum rotu a ɔdze W' besie yie

Dwen papa a ɔye ma wo n'ho (PAN(F) 176

Ama loved the word of God, and one of her favorite Bible verses was Psalm 91. As a Sunday school teacher, Teacher Hannah as she was fondly called, trained a lot of youngsters who are now serving as women and men of the gospel both home and abroad. Hannah loved God indeed and lived life acceptable unto our Lord and master Jesus Christ.

Hannah was a product of the Presbyterian Women Training College (PWTC), Aburi, in the Eastern Region where she obtained a Teacher's Certificate 'A'. Hannah taught at St. John's Anglican Basic School at Nsawam after PWTC. It, therefore, came as no surprise to some of us, when Hannah married the then Elder Philip Osei-Korsah in 2000 after two years of friendship. I remember that at her engagement at the Arakan Junior Ranks MESS, I was so excited, that, I could not hide my joy. Two years into marriage life the couple was called into the full-time ministry of The Church of Pentecost, fulfilling her heart desire of marrying a pastor. She later went for further studies at Winneba, graduating in 2016, with a post-graduate degree in education from the University of Education, Winneba (UEW). Her teaching career saw her work at the following places:

- Asante Apaah Methodist Primary – 2002 to 2003
- Asante Jamasi Methodist Primary – 2003 to 2005
- Kamina Barracks Primary, Tamale – 2005 to 2010
- New Abossey Okai Basic School, Accra – 2010 to 2018
- Apewosika M/A Basic School, Axim - 2018 to 2022

Ama will call and tell me all about marriage life. She told me how on her first night, she and her husband were so naïve, they had no choice but to laugh at themselves. Oh! we would laugh over silly things. We would argue and disagree on issues yet come back to square one. We would stay on the phone for long hours talking about almost everything. We would discuss the education of her girls, their future careers, as Stella, one of her daughters wanted to be a journalist like me. We would laugh at how she would have ended up elsewhere but for Osofo Korsah.

Jamasi in the Ashanti Region was their first station, enroute to Yeji, my hometown. She would call and tell me stories about ministry life, the lows and highs. She carried me along her ministry journey from one area to the other. Distance kept as apart physically, but technology - mobile phone connected us.

Ama lived a life of an ideal pastor's wife through and through. Hannah was hospitable. I remember I led a five-member team from Ghana Broadcasting Corporation GBC, Accra on assignment to the Northern Regional capital Tamale, where she was then stationed. O mine, till date the team members keep asking and talking about her hospitality especially, her culinary skills. Even though I was the only one she knew among the team, she did not discriminate in attending to us. Like Rebecca in the Bible at the well (Genesis 24: 45-47), she fed and accommodated us to the admiration of all. Her doors were opened to all both young and old. The team was shocked to hear of her untimely death.

With the establishment of the Pentecost Convention Center- PCC, we had the opportunity to frequently meet for church programs, with me then as a Media Advisor to the church. We always looked forward to catching up at such meetings no matter how brief. Ama would seize the occasion to proudly introduce me to her colleague Osafomaame, "This is Peggy, my sister, my friend." Because of her, I know a couple of movers and shakers of The church of Pentecost system. Indeed, she was human and had her own limitations, but her positives indeed outweighed her shortcomings. The news of her demise came through on that fateful Monday morning, in the form of a question. "Sister Ama, have you heard of the death of Hannah?" "Which Hannah? Korsah's wife! I screamed, "Who?! Which Korsah? Our Hannah?" "Yes," was the response. No, you are joking right? You get off the phone, I will revert. I made the first call to the church's Headquarters. the gentleman had not heard, but promised to cross check and revert. A few minutes later, he makes good his promise and returns the call with scanty information, "The security man says, they left home early this morning and are yet to return." "No, no, no, wait, let me call Apostle himself." My mind was racing, I placed the call through Apostle's line. O mine, pick up the phone. He does, Osofo, what is happening, what am I hearing? Ama as he calls me, it is true. What is true? Then boom! Are you joking or something? It is not a joke, I am on my way from the hospital, "Ama, Ama is gone." Eii, God is that how you are? Then comes a call from an Elder, Aunty Peggy, please I have heard something, and I want to ask you. He poses same question, so why call me, when you work at the headquarters? O, she told me once, you are sisters, that is why I wanted to know from you. Hmmm, well it is true. My day ended. Now, how do you explain the death of a lady who attended a funeral in the Central Region of Ghana on Saturday, returned to participate in the launch of the church's One Member, One Discipled Soul program at Kaneshie Central of the church a day after- on Sunday who together with her husband were introduced to the gathering at the program, only to wake up early Monday morning with the news that she has passed on to glory? I would have understood if she was involved in an accident, but after a casual complaint of heartache? Do you understand my 'WHY' question? I seek to know if combining her work as a Headmistress of Apewosika MA Basic School in Axim in the Western Region of Ghana and commuting back to the national capital of Accra to visit family and perform ministry work over the weekends was stressful? Could she not make time to rest? Was there an ailment that needed attention she took for granted? There are more questions than answers. Equipped with such, we turn our attention to the question, who is a pastor?

Three

WHO IS A PASTOR?

The 2005, nineth edition of Longman Active Study dictionary defines a pastor, simply as a priest in some Protestant churches. However, on page 16 of the 2008 Ministerial Handbook of The Church of Pentecost, a Pastor, or Minister is said to be a male through whom the ascended Lord governs the Church which is the body of Christ. He is a called worker by the Executive Council with the ratification of the General Council.

Unlike other denominations, where people decide on their own to go into ministry, that cannot be said of The Church of Pentecost. The procedure is different, one may have a desire, but that is just a desire because young men are monitored and recommended, and nobody gets called into ministry without the prior recommendation of the ministerial committee or the Executive Council and the endorsement of the General Council, unless in some exceptional cases which may be determined on a case by cases basis.

As a member of The Church of Pentecost, which the late Hannah Osei-Korsah belonged to, this work looks at the pastor in the CoP by considering the procedure of the CALLING. The call into the full-time ministry starts from the local assembly, through to the district, the area and ends at the national level. When a person in this case a male is identified, the person goes through interviews from the various stages. Once the candidate goes through successfully, the name is issued in a circular letter from the Chairman's office to all assemblies for all to see to avoid any adverse findings against the candidate before acceptance by the Executive Council and afterwards ratified by the General Council.

Though, the successful candidate is interviewed with his wife for ministry at the district and area levels. It is only the candidate (man) who goes for ministerial training and later assigned specific roles. Also, in prescribing the core duties of the minister, which includes but not limited to caring for the flock, teaching and preaching the word, to visit members, bury the dead, dedicate children, interview and bless marriages, not a single official assignment is assigned the pastor's wife, yet she is seen as a co-partner in ministry and must work hand in hand with her husband. What is she then expected to do by way of work? Now that we know who the pastor is, who then is the pastor's wife and what is her official assignment? The next chapter takes this into consideration.

THE PASTOR'S WIFE
AND HER ROLE

As the name suggests, a pastor's wife is simply a lady married to a minister of the gospel. She is the first lady in the home of a pastor and of her congregation. The Bible, however, does not give any explicit teaching about the role of the pastor's wife, but in reading 1 Corinthians 14: 33b-36, Genesis 1:26-28, 2:18, and Proverbs 31:10-31, these scriptures lay Biblical foundations for understanding the role and purpose of women and wives. Implying that, the behavior of any woman in ministry or leadership must conform to that of 1 Timothy 3:11 which suggests that she must be 'worthy of respect'. Moreover, as a wife, she should be praiseworthy, according to Proverbs 31:30.

Kevin Gary Smith in an article, "The Role of the Pastor's Wife, what does the Bible Teach?" cites Leschenne Rebuli's work titled, " The Biblical Role of the Pastor's Wife in the Local church: A case study of churches in Somerset West, Western Cape, says the scriptures do not in any way define or prescribe the role of the pastor's wife. However, we can infer the framework for her ministry as the pastor's wife from what the scripture teaches about her identity, role and purpose as a woman, a wife, and a believer. This, therefore, suggests that she is first a woman designed to reflect her creator and then a wife who ministers to her husband as his helper and finally as a believer who finds her identity in Christ and serves Him according to the gifts and calling He places on her.

Back home to Ghana, in the book, "The Ideal Minister's wife," Gladys Frimpong-Manso, an ordained minister of the Assemblies of God, Ghana and also a pastor's wife, says the pastor's or minister's wife faces an identity crisis in the church, in the sense that she is not sure of who she is in ministry as the pastor's wife. This is because, while some members assume because she is a pastor's wife, she is automatically a pastor by that position. Others think that because she has no formal training like her husband, she is as ordinary as any other church member. Either way, they may be right, she goes on to list some seven qualities of the pastor's wife, namely being born again, filled with the Holy Spirit, God-fearing, well groomed, wise, prudent and virtuous.

In looking at the role or functions of the pastor's wife, she again lists nine key areas every minister's wife ought to possess. This, she gives, as ministering, counselling, role modeling, women's ministry advisor, prayer warrior/intercessor, receiving visitors, leading, resolving conflicts and visitation.

Under ministering, Gladys Frimpong-Manso, says since preaching is the core duty of the pastor, every pastor's wife should be able to preach too. She believes that sometimes, same work could take the pastor away from church and it behooves on the wife to be able to step in, especially when it is a young church. She adds that, the wife can be called upon to preach at any time, hence the need for her to be prepared in and out of season to minister the undiluted word of God to all. She encourages wives to exercise their spiritual giftings and not allow anything to intimidate them, citing Hannah and Mary (1 Samuel 2:1-10, Luke 1:39-59) as examples.

She adds that, a pastor's wife should be in a position to help members overcome or come out of a problem or challenge they encounter by engaging the person in the process. She is quick to say, nonetheless, that this counselling should not be misrepresented to be the giving of advice where the pastor's wife assumes an elderly role of trying to teach the other what to do. Here, she advises that the wife, like the husband, should acquire some basic counselling skills in the sense that no matter what, some people, members and non-members alike, will approach her with some problems, adding that some men even feel comfortable seeking counsel from the pastor's wife than the pastor himself.

Furthermore, the Pastor's Wife should serve as a role model for the young women, married and unmarried. As found in Titus 2:4-8, "Wives, in the same way submit yourselves to your husbands so that, if any of them do not believe the word, they may be won over without words by the behavior of their wives, when they see the purity and reverence of your lives. Your beauty should not come from outward adornment, such as elaborate hairstyles and the wearing of gold jewelry or fine clothes. Rather, it should be that of your inner self, the unfading beauty of a gentle and quiet spirit which is of great worth in God's sight. For this is the way the holy women of the past who put their hope in God used to adorn themselves. They submitted themselves to their husbands" (1 Peter 3:1-6). And so like Sarah, their submission to their husbands will serve as an example for the women in the church. Modesty should be their key word so that their lives would be worthy of emulation.

The Women's Ministry brings the women together for fellowship and also serves as an avenue for spiritual growth. The pastor's wife should be able to offer pieces of advice to the women and also help them in drawing their programs. She should be careful not to dictate to them nor lord herself over them. Her role should be more of unification and also a peacemaker to settle disputes.

The pastor's wife should be a prayer warrior and an intercessor for the husband and the church as a whole. For without prayer she cannot succeed, like any other Christian. She should remember prayer is the key and so should pray without ceasing. (1Thesssalonians 5:17). The pastor's wife should be ready to intercede for all who come to her with issues and challenges and must be involved in all prayer programmes of the church. Together with the leader, they should organize retreats for leadership or sometimes for the presbytery.

Receiving visitors should not be an afterthought for the pastor's wife. The mission house should be opened to all, including family, guest speakers, friends and even strangers like Dorcas and Phoebe did. (Romans 16:1-2, Acts 9:36). She should be able to help those in need and not always expect to receive. This part of ministry, Gladys Frimpong Manso says though difficult, must not be underrated. Strangely, some visitors will come unannounced at times when the pastor and wife could also be going through their own financial challenges. This is where grace is needed most for financial support.

The pastor's wife should be a leader, by virtue of her being a pastor's wife. As a co-leader with her husband, she needs to go to God in prayer for guidance and through daily reading of the word of God. She must learn from her husband and be able to influence the congregation and serve as a good example. She ought to be a servant leader. This can be learnt from the sinful woman with the alabaster jar who served Jesus with her precious gift (Luke 7: 37-50).

Resolving conflicts according to the author is one of the difficult roles of the pastor's wife, as it involves intellect, will and emotions. She must start this from within, that is solving intra conflicts which may be bitterness she may harbor against her husband and other people. In doing this she must learn to forgive as Christ forgives us (1 Peter 3:8-9, Ephesians 4: 31-32). Then she has to settle inter conflicts within the women's ministry, marriages, friends and families. All this can only be done if she bears the fruit of the Spirit (Galatians 5:22). Here she needs divine wisdom and this can be gotten through prayer.

On Visitation, Mrs. Frimpong-Manso advises that the Pastor's wife visits with her husband or the women leaders and not to go alone. She ought to be careful with whatever she says during such visits and her conversations should be that of edification. It is wise and proper to start such visitations with prayer, then a brief exhortation from the word of God and if possible, a token gift. The time of visit should be selected carefully and not at odd hours. It is in her interest to give feedback to her husband during times he is not part of the visit. This visitation should not be limited to just the well to do. It is, however, impossible to visit all church members with huge numbers. In the light of this, the pastor's wife should undertake proper planning and be strategic about it. Under no circumstances, should she and her visitation team create any negative impression about selectivity.

Minister Frimpong-Manso continues that the pastor's wife occupies a very weighty place in God's plan for the church and, therefore, she should seek God's help to act in that capacity effectively. And this is where the late Hannah and her colleagues come in. So, in order not to be seen as not playing any role, the pastor's wife, depending on her strength, and background, zooms into work with the women's ministry and warms into the children, then on and on she goes. She once in a while gets the opportunity to preach and also serves as a counselor in some situations. With most of them taking interest in grooming bachelors and spinsters.

In the nutshell, the pastor's wife, is first a "woman" a wife, a believer who mirrors her Creator and helps her husband to win souls to populate heaven and depopulate hell. With this in mind, we want to know how the pastor's wife is known in the four church denominations considered in this book.

Five

TERMINOLOGIES USED FOR PASTORS' WIVES

From one tree - Jesus Christ, Christianity takes on different denominations with different ideologies yet end at the cross as the spring board. Even though with some similarities, there still exist some number of variations from church to church. In most Ghanaian churches, Twi, one of the Akan dialects is widely used, hence most terminologies have Twi roots, a typical example being the term used for the pastor's wife where they derive their titles from. Below are some of the terminologies used in referring to them in the denominations used in this book.

In the Presbyterian Church of Ghana, and the Methodist Church Ghana, the pastor's wife is simply known as Asafomaame, derived from two Twi words -Asafo- congregation and maame -mother, the two put together give us Asafomaame or mother of the congregation.

On their part, Assemblies of God, Ghana uses Osofo Maame – mother of the Pastor as is used in The

Church of Pentecost. However, as the Assemblies of God Ghana, embarks on its rebranding drive under the current General Superintendent, Rev. Dr. Stephen Yenusom Wengam, it is not known if the name Osofo maame will be maintained.

In some Charismatic churches, like the International Central Gospel Church (ICGC), a member of the Ghana Pentecostal and Charismatic Council (GPCC), a pastor's wife has no special name, however, the Founder's wife is known as **Lady** Joy, and in some branches the members on their own decide to add lady to the first name of the pastor's wife, whiles others simply say, Mama as a sign of respect.

In The Church of Pentecost, where the late Osofo Maame, Hannah Osei-Korsah worshipped, they are officially known as Osofo Maame- the pastor's mother, something oral history suggests was learnt from the other churches. In recent times, however, some members have started referring to them as Asafo Maame, which stands for mother of the church.

In considering the various terminologies, we would now take the views of some of the finest brains in Christendom in Ghana, West Africa, the setting of this book.

Six

VIEWS FROM OUR FATHERS

Experts recommend the need for consultation in any undertaking, as it does not only give one just a better understanding, but also gives variation and credence to whatever one might be doing. In writing about who a pastor's wife is and what her role(s) are, views from some of the finest fathers of the gospel who have walked and continue to walk in the Lord made time to share their views. Let me be quick to mention that, some shared their viewpoints from their denominations whiles others shared their personal standpoints.

"The Pastor's Wife is commonly known as Osofomaame in The Church of Pentecost. In making recommendations to improve upon the role of the Pastor's Wife, I want to say that pastors' wives should be considered as they are wives of pastors. They should not be involved in too many meetings and activities. They can be left to practice their professions, since they are not officially ordained as paid pastors. Once the unfortunate issue of dismissals take place, the wives are also 'dismissed.' They should also not take the roles of women leaders. Women leaders are often reviewed but pastors' wives are not. They should complement one another. Pastors' wives should do what they can, and not be coerced to do what they cannot. The qualification of a lady at the time of call of her husband into ministry should not be an issue. I believe that not all ladies are called as ministers of the gospel, and so, ministry should not be full time for all. New entrants should consider the import of the ministry before coming into it, and not only look at the fringe benefits."

Apostle Prof. Opoku Onyinah – Former Chairman, The Church of Pentecost. He served in the vine yard of the Lord for forty-two years and went on voluntary retirement at age sixty-four, a year earlier than the mandated years of sixty-five.

"In the Methodist Church, we do not have Pastor's Wife, but Minister's Spouse. This is because both men and women can be Ministers. The women are called Asofomaame and the men are called Asofopapa." To make it easier for all, the church has an association called the Minister's Spouse Association for the two groups. Since most female ministers are engaged in other professions, the church does not insist on the spouse engaging in full time ministry. They are however encouraged to support their spouses. To improve upon the role of spouses in the Methodist Church, there is the need for the Church to organize workshops and conferences to equip them to learn about the changing dynamics of the ministry and home. Such a forum would assist in keeping the home and combining their professions and ministry. I encourage spouses to be on top of the new dynamics of the Church and ministry. The times and understanding of ministry is changing, and so the spouses must add value to themselves. They must be strategic in the support they give to the members and their families. They should realise that being a minister's spouse is a calling from God, because it has many privileges and responsibilities. A spouse must have a big heart to support just like the minister/pastor."

Most Rev. Dr. Paul Kwabena Boafo, Presiding Bishop, Methodist Church, Ghana. As at the time of writing this book, he had served the Methodist Church, Ghana for thirty-seven years as a minister of the gospel.

In addition to serving as the wife of the pastor, the Pastor's Wife is expected to assist the pastor in his ministry. The name 'Osofo Maame' or 'Asafo Maame' is used inter-changeably to refer to the Pastor's Wife in Assemblies of God, Ghana. I think, it is important to consider the qualification of the "lady" before they get called into ministry. For me, as to whether an Asafomaame should do full-time ministry depends on the ideology of the church. Nonetheless, it is the duty of all pastors' wives to support the work of their husbands. I recommend "The Ideal Minister's Wife" authored by Gladys Frimpong-Manso for all pastors' wives to read to improve upon their roles and also for new entrants into ministry.

Immediate past General Superintendent, Assemblies of God, Ghana. Rev Prof. Paul Frimpong-Manso.

I personally think, considering the qualification of the lady before calling the husband into ministry is necessary, I support the idea that a pastor's wife should do full-time ministry. However, she can engage in her secular employment and still support her husband's ministry. She should be discouraged from engaging in any employment that takes her away from her husband's duty station. For example, it is unacceptable for her to be working in Accra when her husband is stationed at Tamale. For this reason, they are made to sign a commitment and consent form before their husbands are interviewed for consideration into the full-time ministry. Those who are unable to make that commitment are usually asked to exercise their ministries outside the full-time ministry.

To improve upon the role of the pastor's wife in The Church of Pentecost, I cite the example of Priscilla and Aquilla, and I advise they should team up with their husbands to get the work done and continue to trust that the Lord who has called will take care of them. For that reason, they should bring all their giftings to bear on their husband's ministry. New entrants should remain committed to the ministry of the church and their husband's ministry in the assurance that the Lord will never make them worse off in the long term. Indeed, from the history of the Church, I have not seen any pastor and his wife who have been made worse off after serving the church faithfully and diligently.

Apostle Dr. Alfred Koduah - Former General Secretary, of The Church of Pentecost. He retired in 2021 as the Area Head of the church in the Teshie Nungua Area, after serving the Lord as Minister for thirty-seven years.

It is mandatory for a minister in The Church of Pentecost to marry before they are ordained into the full-time ministry, hence their spouses are referred to as pastors' wives. In The CoP, since the wife is not the front-line person in ministry, their academic qualification is not strictly considered, and secondly, they could sail through ministry without academic demands. That, notwithstanding, if they are educated, it enhances their ministry in terms of knowledge acquisition and articulate communication. The current arrangement, which makes it optional for them is preferable, as not all ministers' wives have the capacity for effective ministry. Therefore, to ask someone to do full-time ministry, to which she may not be well disposed, would only frustrate her. Efforts should be made to identify their special interest in ministry. Whilst some may be well disposed to the children's ministry, others may, for instance, be interested in counseling. This will help them develop capacity and pursue their interest within the scope of ministry. I recommend they should be exposed to on-service training regarding their role in ministry, such as housekeeping, catering and hospitality. Their dual roles as mothers at home and in the church can be enhanced if they learn more about child-psychology and human relations. Exposing pastors' wives to lectures in emotional intelligence would help them develop capacity to relate well to church members and help others who may be experiencing relationship problems.

Since the position of the pastors' wives in the church is contingent upon their husbands' roles, they should be concerned about the man's health and good housekeeping and also do well to appreciate the members, even if some of them are difficult to manage. Learning basic principles of time management and the ability to prioritize is key in ministry.

New female entrants, should tame their expectations of the ministry and should understand that ministry is a sacrificial venture and also learn to appreciate and relate well to people of varied backgrounds and attitudes. Also, they should learn to be discreet and confidential and also learn to be grateful to the members for every gift and support, no matter how little.

Apostle Dr. Dela Quampah, Area Head, Ho and Executive Council Member. He was a former National Head of The Church of Pentecost, South Africa.

Having read views from some of our fathers and generals of the gospel, we turn our attention to the pastors' wives themselves, to find out exactly what they make of their "calling" and the encouragement or advise they have for young ladies who aspire to become pastors' wives.

VIEWS FROM SOME PASTORS' WIVES

I n this chapter, we will read views from thirty-five pastors' wives from different denominations from both home and abroad. As stated earlier, every denomination has a different title for the pastor's wife, it ranges from Asafomaame, Lady and Osofomaame. Note, these are their personal experiences and not a representation of their churches. It is meant to serve as a guide and insight to their roles and activities.

She has a B.Sc. in Optometry and Visual Sciences, Doctor of Optometry and Masters in Clinical Psychology. She married at twenty-four, and two years into marriage, they were called into the full-time ministry in The Church of Pentecost, a role she has been playing for the past fourteen years. In her own words, "My role as a pastor's wife is to fulfill God's purpose for my life (impact lives in ways that expands the kingdom of God and brings glory to God). God has yoked this purpose with that of my husband. Thus, as a pastor's wife, I partner my husband to achieve maximum output in what God has called him to do. My role is to provide a safe space for my husband to vent, brainstorm, and question his progress or goals, yet encouraging and supporting the vision God has given him. Many pastors do not have close friends with whom they can vent or share their problems (due to trust and confidentiality issues). A pastor's wife provides that companionship that encourages her husband. This has been a critical learning experience. As a pastor's wife, though I am not necessarily employed by the church, I whole heartedly utilize my God-given gifts to volunteer in different areas of ministry. This, I do, cheerfully as a Christian to serve God, my husband and family and the congregation where we serve."

Touching on the challenges of a pastor's wife in her denomination, Dr. lists adapting to different duty stations and helping people to understand the nature of full-time ministry. Responding to the issue of fashion and the pastor's wife assumed selectivity in relating to church members, she said it may not be entirely true. She explained that sometimes, your closeness to people who spur you unto good works, points out genuine weakness you may have. Appreciating your grace and callings may portray the perception of being selective. She says the pastor's wife ought to consciously relate with all members in a kind and supportive way. She is quick to add however that, she would not totally discount that perception, if it is based on experience as some people may have genuinely experienced discrimination for one reason or the other.

Her Saturdays are used to coordinate youth ministry activities for the nation in which they serve. And those are the days when the youth and youth leaders are available for planning youth services, outdoor programs, preparing church auditorium for services, visitations among others, making the day her busiest. She believes that a good balance between spiritual, marital, and family, career, social and ecclesiastical roles will make her more effective for kingdom advancement.

Dr. has no regrets at all as a pastor's wife, saying it has been a great springboard for massive growth in her marital, spiritual, social, and intellectual domains of her life. "Being a pastor's wife helped me understand that purpose is impacting lives in ways that expands the kingdom of God and manifests the glory of God. Thus, ministry is just one of the means to do that. It becomes even "easier" when one's husband has this understanding or insight and tugs the wife along in a gracious way." Her advice to ladies who want or would be married to pastors is to pray for themselves to have understanding into the calling and pray same for their husbands. Ministry, she says, is understanding who you are as a Christian and touching lives effortlessly by God's grace.

Lady YG at the time of writing was stationed at Abor in the Volta Region of Ghana. She is a thirty-seven-year-old degree holder and belongs to The Apostolic Church, Ghana. Her parents are not ministers of the gospel. She married at age twenty-eight. Her dream was to marry a pastor, so when ministry life came after marriage, she took it with all seriousness and has been at it for the past two years, serving as a pillar for her husband and a mother figure to the church and the community.

Over this period, she has identified unrealistic expectations from some members as her main challenge.

Lady YG, says, "It is false for anyone to think ministry is all about dressing or fashion." She nonetheless agrees that some are selective in associating with some church members whom they cannot afford to go deeper than "small talks" with them due to their nature. And as a career woman, a mother, and a pastor's wife, Saturdays and Sundays are her busiest days, especially the latter for obvious reasons. She recommends frequent custom-made training programs as measures to make her and her colleagues more effective for kingdom advancement. She calls on young ladies who are considering ministry not to desire to marry a pastor for the fame or money. For her, frequent sensitization for all congregants on the work/role of a pastor's wife will help all.

Obaa Yaa is thirty-nine years old and has an MBA in Human Resource Management. Currently, stationed in the Eastern Region of Ghana. She married at twenty-six years without any opposition from her parents to a public servant before they were called into the full-time ministry of The Church of Pentecost and has served in that capacity for eleven years.

Obaa Yaa serves as a role model impacting the lives of the female congregants. She sees herself as a prayer warrior and an organizer of the women. She says ministry goes beyond fashion. She is neither discriminatory nor selective in her association with church members, but Obaa believes it is an individual's nature to do otherwise. Ministry for Obaa comes with some challenges. The ability to handle other people's concerns amicably without altering the church and people's lives are her concerns. As a career woman, her busiest days are during the weekends as they come with social functions such as weddings and funerals. She suggests and recommends that pastors' wives ought to be prayerful and learn new things in an ever-changing world. She has no regrets going into ministry with her husband and advices new entrants to know they have been selected by God, and so remain worthy of the sacred calling.

Growing up, Akua's heart desire had always been to marry a pastor. Graciously, she married at age thirty-four and became an Osofomaame a couple of years later in The Church of Pentecost. She and her husband are currently based in Ghana's capital, Accra. With a Master's degree, she has been a pastor's wife for the past eighteen years. She serves as a role model for the women, counselor, preacher and teaches the word of God alongside praying for the work of God and seeking the welfare of members especially, women. As a career woman, she combines her regular workload with that of ministry, making it difficult for her to make time for herself. She has no privacy and members' expectation of an excellent character from her is a headache. Akua's busiest days are the weekends when the days are fully packed with programs. She has no time to discriminate or be selective in relating to members as she sees all as children of the kingdom.

Even though Akua has no regrets with ministry life, she recommends and suggests that "Our careers must be acknowledged and be given space to go on with our plans." This is her message to the up and coming; "They should know that it is a call to do kingdom business and not just to dress fashionably." She ends by saying, "Pastors' wives augment the pastor's work, and they, therefore, ought to be given equal treatment as is given to the pastors."

From the Presbyterian Church of Ghana, LML is located at North Kaneshie in Accra. She is a postgraduate degree holder and is forty-four years old. She is from a "non-ministerial" home and had no opposition marrying her husband. She had always wanted to marry a pastor and God blessed her with a pastor at age thirty-eight. She has served in that role for six years now. LML says she is first and foremost, a minister to her husband and then supports the Women's Fellowship. She says she faces the usual challenges faced by the average spouse. As a career woman and a pastor's wife, she thinks the notion that some of them are selective and discriminatory towards members, is an outgrowth of one's personality. She adds that some people are outgoing whilst others are not. "You just need to know your personality and manage it."

For LML, Sundays are her busiest. This is because, not only is she a wife and mother, but she is also a pastor's wife at church and by extension church mother. Her life goes beyond dressing or fashion. She has no regrets serving as a pastor's wife, adding that it is a ministry worth pursing with fulfilling results. She advises those in and those coming in to see it as such. Summing up: "I enjoy being a pastor's spouse. I wouldn't choose any other."

From the United States of America comes forty-five-year-old GAA. She is a trained broadcast journalist and tops it up with a Bachelor of Science degree in Nursing. She has been a pastor's wife in The Church of Pentecost for the past decade. She married at twenty-five with no opposition from her parents and became a pastor's wife along the way. As a full-time pastor's wife, she has a tall list of roles, including being able to develop personal and intimate relationship with God. She supports, prays for/with, and partners with her husband in ministry work. "Home management and nurturing duties for my husband and children is a constant." She is a spiritual mother to the congregation, provides hospitality, counseling, and mentorship to the membership as and when needed. She prays for the wellbeing of the work of ministry and the congregation, among others. Top on the list of the challenges she faces are feelings of inadequacy, loneliness, and carrying the weight of the heavy burdens of members in prayer for breakthroughs during midnight hours.

Discrimination and selectiveness are out of her vocabulary. Due to her involvement with the Youth Ministry and Pentecost International Worship Centre (PIWC), her doors are open to all. Lady GAA says her relationship and interactions with the church membership are very cordial and without formalities. She notes that to be more effective for kingdom advancement, pastors' wives must understand that they are accountable to God (who called them) and the church. Therefore, "your life should be worthy of your calling. You must endeavor to serve God and man with a cheerful heart."

New entrants, hear her in this admonition: "Feelings of inadequacy and loneliness might surface sometimes, but remember, our sufficiency is of God (2 Corinthians 3:5). So, draw near to God who equips us, and develop a deep intimacy with the Holy Spirit, who is our helper."

She concludes that although life as a pastor's wife is fulfilling, it can also be daunting at times. However, the consolation is that God who has called is faithful, and He will sustain, and accomplish His purpose in our lives!!

A Pentecostal from the Assemblies of God, Ghana, PA resides in Kasoa and is thirty-eight years old. The degree holder is a daughter of ministers of the gospel and married at age twenty-five without any problems from them. She has always wanted to marry a pastor, unfortunately, it was not until three years ago that she became an Asafomaame. PA plays the role of a mother to the church, an advisor to the Women's Movement, a counsellor, and a youth advocate. Again, she serves as an advisor and prayer warrior to her husband. Within three years of ministry, she identifies envy, spiritual and physical attacks as her main challenges. For PA, it is an outright no for anyone to say ministry for asafomaame is all about fashion/dressing. Answering the question on asafomaame selectiveness in relating with church members, she had this to say, "I love all, but the Bible says we should be wise like the serpent."

The thirty-eight-year-old career mother lists three out of the seven days of the week as her busiest Mondays, Wednesdays, and Fridays. This is because those days are church activity days, and by her position, she has to close from work and still go to church to honor God. For effectiveness in ministry, RA says pastors' wives need to be more prayerful. Currently, she has no regrets in ministry. Her advise to young ladies who want to go into ministry is that they should take their relationships with God more seriously.

From the Bono East Region of Ghana, TK is a thirty-five year old trained teacher who married at twenty-five to the love of her youth before she was called into full time ministry. Her major role for the past five years has been to support her husband spiritually as a prayer warrior and physically by making sure he is always in a good mood to welcome his congregation and visitors. "Hmmm, the work is not about dressing or fashion, it is a call and if you are not mature in Christ, you can't do it. If it were about dressing and fashion, some of us will not be called. We are not selective; it is about the relationship between you and the members." Though a professional teacher, TK is now a full-time pastor's wife. She recounts an incidence in which she was once involved in a motor accident with her seven-month-old baby which has affected her health. In spite of this, she has never regretted for working in the Lord's vineyard. "My little advice to my sisters coming into ministry is to let prayer be their food and let the grace of God lead them." Doing ministry in an internal missions' area, TK says her busiest days are Sundays and Mondays. These two days are when most members who are traders come from the island and surrounding communities to trade. "My recommendation and suggestions can be found in Ephesians 6: 7, "Serve wholeheartedly, as if you were serving the Lord not men."

EOF lives in Dambai in the Oti Region of Ghana. She married at twenty-seven. A graduate from one of Ghana's tertiary institutions, has been a pastor's wife for ten years. She is not from a minister of God's family, yet had no opposition with marrying her husband. They were called into the full-time ministry of The Church of Pentecost after marriage. She helps her husband by supporting the Women's Ministry. She feels limited to certain things and always under some kind of "unseen law." As a full-time pastor's wife, she says ministry is not about fashion. She believes in the notion that as a human institution, some could be selective and discriminatory. "Being a pastor's wife is a calling and comes with a lot of responsibilities, so you shouldn't force your husband to be in ministry if it is not the will of God or else you will regret later." EOF says because it is God who called them, He is able to see them through faithfully if only they remain in him faithfully.

Marrying at age twenty-eight years, forty-five years old Mrs. EA is based in Accra, Ghana. She is a graduate from a tertiary institution. Her parents are not ministers of the gospel, but she had a smooth sail through marriage. Ministry came later on in marriage in The Apostolic Church, Ghana, and she has been in it for the past twelve years. As a pastor's wife, she assists her husband in the running of the church. She undertakes counselling and draws program outlines for Sundays. As a life coach, her heartbeat is ensuring that the youth become better versions of themselves. For Mrs EA, challenges come in different forms- "Members not following your vision, lack of commitment and sitting on the fence by some members." She puts it bluntly that it is false for anyone to think their preoccupation as pastors' wives is fashion or dressing. "As a church mother, you have to be sociable but you have to set limits and so cannot afford to be selective."

As a career woman, Mrs. EA's weekends are extremely busy, because there is always either a wedding, naming or christening, funeral and series of meetings to attend. She has no regrets so far for marrying a pastor. She suggests empowerment programs should be organized frequently for them to upgrade themselves for an effective ministry life. Her advice to the upcoming ones is to be more prayerful, adding, "Fashion is good, but it shouldn't be overdone."

She calls on leadership to consider empowering the pastor's wife through training. "When a pastor is called, I think that the wife has also been called, so any training the pastor goes through, like the Bible school, the wife should also attend."

She is a Minister's daughter; her marriage did not suffer any setbacks. They became Ministers of the gospel in The Church of Pentecost after marriage and have been serving in that role for the past eight years. At fifty, they are currently located in the Central Region. She holds a Master of Art degree. Mary serves as a counselor to the women and assist the Women's Ministry alongside the occasional preaching assignments. "Time to balance my work as a classroom teacher and to attend Ministers' Wives meetings and church programs at the same time is my challenge."

On the issue of selectiveness and discrimination, she says though it is not entirely true, it has to do with individual differences. She is firm in her view that the notion that some pastors' wives are deep into fashion consciousness cannot be true. As a classroom teacher, she is always busy Monday through Friday.

She encourages new entrants to be familiar with activities in the various ministries within the Church to avoid any embarrassment whenever they are called upon to minister or play a role as a minister's wife. To make them more effective for kingdom advancement, "I recommend pastors' wives are put on payroll. Higher authorities should consider and encourage us especially career wives, to render our services in the communities and, the nation at large."

Lady V is fifty-four years old and serves in the Presbyterian Church of Ghana. She is now stationed at Aburi in the Eastern Region of Ghana. Her dream was to marry a pastor, but it was not until after ten years of marriage that she became an Asafomaame and has been married for eighteen years now. She had a smooth preparation into marriage, without any opposition.

Mama V says her position does not place any special role on her in her church apart from complementing her husband by offering him the necessary support spiritually and physically. As a professional teacher, she gets preaching opportunities and utilizes her talent in the children's department as a children's service teacher, something she has been doing since she married.

Even though she has no regrets being a pastor's wife, the challenge of being above reproach and serving as a role model to both young and old, married and unmarried weighs heavily on her. As a career woman, putting the house in order for the ensuing week through cooking and washing among others makes Saturdays her busiest day in the week.

Reacting to the perception that ministry is all about fashion, Mama V says it is false. She has tried over the years to be down to earth and affable to all manner of persons and cannot be described among those who are selective if any at all because "being a pastor's wife changes one overnight." She recommends that regular training programs be organized for spouses to make them effective so they will be able to address contemporary issues that confront them. For the young ladies considering marrying pastors, Mrs. VB opines, "If they are not ready to see themselves as instruments to be used together with their husbands to advance kingdom business, then they should not come into ministry." Mama VB observes that in certain congregations in the Presbyterian Church of Ghana, pastors' wives sit among members, while she can sit with the Session up front. She is of the view that when they sit among the Session, they would be in a better position to prompt their husbands when the need be.

Without any hurdles, Eve married at twenty-two to a pastor in The Church of Pentecost. Now, thirty-two, she is a tertiary school graduate, and has served as an Osofomaame for the past ten years as at 2023. Based in Eastern Region, Mama Eve says her role in these years has been praying and supporting her husband from behind. As a career woman, her challenges include, the notion that she enjoys the church's money. Sundays are her busiest. Trusting God and prayers are her recommendations for effective advancement of Kingdom business. She adds that it is not true that fashion is their concern and they are not selective in choosing friends among members. Evelyn has no regrets for marrying a pastor. She calls on young ladies considering ministry life to rely on God in everything when they get that opportunity.

Even though she is a daughter of a Minister of The Church of Pentecost, Jo, a tertiary degree holder had no desire to marry a pastor. Without any hurdles she married at age thirty. Seven years into her marriage, she and her husband got called into the same ministry of her parents. Now at forty-three, Jo resides at Asamankese in the Eastern part of Ghana.

As a full-time pastor's wife, Jo's sole role is to "support my husband in every aspect of ministry." Jo is always busy and that is her main challenge. She suggests periodic workshops for the training of pastors' wives for effective kingdom advancement. She says being a pastor's wife is a high and noble calling which all females must desire. Jo debunks the notion of fashion and selectiveness of friends among church members with regards to pastors' wives as false. For her, the weekends are her busiest.

The thirty-one-year-old diploma holder, became an osofomaame of The Church of Pentecost some years ago. EB's main challenge as a pastor's wife is not having access to some social amenities due to where they find themselves currently. Even though she had no desire marrying a pastor, she has no regrets going into ministry with her husband. Combining ministry with her career, has not been easy. For now, she is preoccupied with helping her husband fulfill his ministry. She does not agree with the assertion that Asafomaame are selective in associating with church members or that they are fashion-conscious. She advises her colleagues never to be selective in dealing with church members. She adds, "Young ladies are to know that it is a calling not a fashion show."

GAA, a Presbyterian Asafomaame, serves at New Bortianor in the Greater Accra Region. Now, fifty-seven years, she is twenty- eight years in marriage of which twenty has been spent in the ministry. She has an Ordinary Level General Certificate Examination (GCE) Certificate. She works as a preacher, a marriage counselor and advisor. She taught in the children service for fifteen years and currently teaches new converts' class. She doubles as a prayer warrior and uses her Thursdays for house-to-house evangelism in her community. She says as a pastor's wife, "people in the church and the community criticize you wrongly, not just you but your husband and children. Members are watching your steps, and it gets challenging when you are criticized. If you assist your husband too much or if you do not do enough, people will still criticize you. The other challenge is that as a pastor's wife, when you have issues or problems even with your husband, you have nobody to talk to or advice you."

As a career wife, Saturdays are her busiest especially when there are funerals, weddings from both family and church members as well as within the community, as she gets invited. Again, on some Sundays, when she has to take would-be couples through counseling, this she does after church service before finally attending to the kitchen.

She is of the opinion that some pastors' wives are selective, but thinks the bit on fashion is false. She says to err is human and to forgive divine, so Asafomaame should also be shown leniency when they go wrong. Like all others, she has no regrets being a pastor's wife, as she sees it as a calling. "My message to young ladies who want to be pastors' wives is that it is not a guarantee that you will go to heaven, rather your good deeds." She adds, "Know your calling, that God has a special work that He wants you to do for Him." She calls on them not to discriminate but rather, love all, be approachable, be prayerful, wear a smiling face all the time, be a responsible person, be ready to serve and not to be served (Romans 12:9-18). She concludes by saying, "Remember, you are Asafomaame but not Osofomaame, and work within your range." GAA thanks the Almighty God for calling her into ministry to serve and not to be served.

From the United States of America, Mama SHE married at age twenty-five. At forty-four, she became Osofo Maame in The Church of Pentecost, some eight years ago.

"As a mother to the church, I assist with anything I can. I am a teacher, a preacher, and a hostess, among others." SHE has a full plate of activities; "It is always about the children, church, and others. I really need to make time to take care of myself. I have so much to do that I hardly take time off to do me."

With a postgraduate degree, the full-time pastor's wife says she cannot speak for every Osofomaame, when it comes to selectivity and fashion. She, however, believes about ninety percent of ministry is about relationship, hence building a good relationship with all members helps you as a minister's wife to reach your members, meet their needs and help in whichever way you can.

Her Saturdays are the busiest, since most social gatherings are held on this day, and she needs to be present all the time amidst scheduled visits and taking care of the home. She adds that as an Osofomaame, you need to develop the "mother's mindset," where you learn to love all your "children" regardless of how "naughty" they may be. You need to be approachable and very involved in your husband's ministry.

She has no regrets being in ministry, but wished she knew one thing before she became a pastor's wife which is "the level of expectation required of you." People will hold you to some pretty high standards, they expect so much from you and expect you to know and act better always."

Hear her all young ladies who aspire to marry pastors. "The pastor's wife role is a calling in itself. You need to allow God to prune you and prepare you for that role. Be ready to invest in prayer in order to be an effective pastor's wife."

JMO, an electrical engineer, had always wanted to be a pastor's wife, a calling that came after marriage. She currently lives and serves in The Church of Pentecost at Kasoa in the Central Region of Ghana. Marrying at age twenty-eight, she has been in ministry for the past eighteen years and is now forty-seven years. She does not have many challenges discharging her role as a partner in her husband's ministry. As a full-time pastor's wife, her weekends are packed with activities such as weddings and funerals.

For JMO, it is false when people claim they have limited ministry to fashion or dressing, and it cannot be true they are selective in associating with church members. "Pray always, study the word of God at all times, fasting, commitment, humility, love for all etc are my suggestions and recommendations to make one more effective for kingdom advancement." She has no regrets for ministry life. She ends by saying, "The Good Lord will help the young ladies in ministry."

Flo is forty-seven years old and lives in the Eastern Region. She has Basic Education Certificate (BECE). She simply calls herself a Christian who had always wanted to be a pastor's wife. She married at twenty-nine years and has been serving as a pastor's wife for the past ten years.

"Organizing the Women's Ministry and assisting my husband in ministry is my passion as a wife of a pastor. As a housewife, in this case and as a full-time pastor's wife, finances are my challenge." Sundays are her busiest days due to church activities and other house chores as well as children's club meetings. "I am not fashion minded neither am I selective in terms of associating with members." Flo thinks some form of training and prayer would make her more effective for Kingdom advancement. She has no regrets marrying a pastor and recommends that "Asofomaame who has no source of income should be given some financial support."

Mama Connie has been in ministry for the past 17 years after marrying at twenty-four and has since been complementing her husband in ministry. A second cycle graduate, forty-six-year-old Mama Connie is an Osofomaame in The Church of Pentecost, and now stations in the Eastern Region. As a full-time church mother, Saturday is her busiest day in the week. She uses the day for cleaning and attending social events like weddings and funerals. She mentions not having enough time for her children and the disorganization of her children's school programs during transfers as her main challenges in ministry.

Mama Connie recommends some form of monthly allowances to complement the home for ministers' wives. This, she believes, will make her more effective for kingdom advancement.

For Connie, ministry goes beyond dressing and no room for selectivity with regards to relating to members. To new entrants, she says, "If it is not your calling, don't rush into it."

Ruthie of The Apostolic Church, Ghana is now a resident of Ave-Dakpa in the Volta Region. Marrying at thirty, she says ministry was not a do or die affair for her. She became a church mother or asafomaame at age thirty-four, which was four years into marriage. Since then, she has been supporting her husband in his ministerial work. She puts her challenges this way, "Hmmm, a lot - time stress - because you want to finish one thing and do another, coping with people and their sayings, etc."

Touching on fashion and dressing, she says it is false and adds that when it comes to selective association with members, it is relative as it is not same with all ministers' wives. She continues by saying that at times, the pastor's wife needs to save herself from some problems and this could account for that perception. The career wife mentions Tuesdays and Saturdays as her busiest days. She uses her time after work on Tuesday for cooking, attending women's meetings which she is often the facilitator and uses the Saturdays for all other house chores. Ruthie, thinks three things; being herself, loving God and His work will make her more effective for Kingdom advancement.

So far, she has no regrets in the ministry, and she calls on those yearning to become pastors' wives not to be afraid, but to sincerely love God and His work and they can do it. She recommends that the church should support pastors' wives financially, adding that the current situation where the pastors receive all the attention be looked at again.

At thirty-eight, Enyo Sarp has been married for ten years now. A graduate from a tertiary institution, she was only six years into ministry at the time of this book. She is currently based in the Eastern Regional capital of Koforidua. For Enyo, supporting her husband to execute his ministerial vision is her role in the scheme of affairs. Over the period, her challenge has been, "Sometimes you don't get to live with your children due to poor social amenities in transfer areas." Enyo is a career woman, so cooking for the week and hosting visitors on Saturdays keep her busiest. She thinks it may be true that some pastors' wives are selective in relating to some church members. "It may be true for some people although that behavior must be condemned. We must embrace all people and show them the love that we received from Christ." Though her parents are not ministers of the gospel she had no issues marrying a pastor. She rejects the view that fashion has become the order of the day for the Asafomaame.

Sar had other plans for her life, but ministry at age thirty-one. Now, forty-three years old, she has been in the vineyard of the Lord for twelve years. The graduate Osofomaame of The Church of Pentecost resides in the Central Region of Ghana. As a full time Osofomaame, she is a pillar beside her husband, and also sees to the needs of women and other groups in the church and relays them to her husband for the needed attention.

"High expectations from members and family, coping with criticisms and opposition to our work, and not getting quick results when starting a new ministry" are the challenges associated with her role as an Osofomaame. On Sundays Sar gets to church early and gets home late making it her busiest day. On selectivity in relating to church members, she thinks that, naturally clicks cannot be avoided, but we are conscious to associate with all members. Otherwise, we are tagged as being discriminatory. Touching on being exceptionally fashion-conscious, Sar says it is false. She suggests more practical training for pastors' wives will make them more effective for kingdom advancement.

Maame Sar advises young ladies who want to marry pastors to be very serious with their spiritual lives, since they are the pillars beside the pastor.

Born to ministers of the gospel, she made the right choice and so Maa 'U' became an Osofomaame a year into marriage, something she had always wanted to be. Now, fifty years, she married at age thirty-two and she is eighteen years into ministry.

Maa 'U' is the pillar beside her husband, A full-time Osofomaame, she has a diploma in Early Childhood Education, and lives in Accra, where she uses her Mondays for prayer time with the women's ministry. Ill-health poses as her main challenge in ministry. Osofomaame 'U' does not hold the belief that she and her colleagues are selective in associating with members and ministry is not about fashion.

She calls on young ladies who want to marry pastors to make time to pray, and work hard for God, adding that it is all about prayers.

In 2004, A.M.A. and her husband were called into the full-time ministry of The Church of Pentecost. Now, a little over fifty-three years, she married at age twenty-two. AMA holds a BSc in Administration with a Human Resource option, a Diploma in Public Relations and a certificate in Marketing, and lives at Kasoa in the Central Region. As a pastor's wife, A M A outlines her role as complementing her husband in the discharge of his duties, alongside being a mother, counsellor, teacher, friend, mentor, spiritual sensor, prayer partner and listening ear for members. She also serves as an encourager and resource person to mention but a few. In short, "I become whatever is needed when the need arises."

Challenges associated with her life as a pastor's wife, include but not limited to: being strong for all, meeting the physical and financial needs of others when you also have needs, loneliness, stress, being misunderstood and taken for granted sometimes, letting go of dreams and careers, having to quickly change emotions, adjusting to various locations and people when previous ones are still not forgotten, backbiting and unintended offenses.

AMA believes that the church, being a human institution, it is possible some Asofomaame may be selective in associating with members, but she is quick to add that she personally thinks it is improper. She says some people themselves label the Osofomaame before they even get to know them. She says it is false for some to say ministry for the Osofomaame is all about dressing and fashion.

As a Full-time Osofomaame, she said she is fulfilled when one's gifts are fully deployed for the Kingdom work, even if they have no official responsibility.

In conclusion, Osofomaame AMA has this for young ladies who also want to marry pastors: "Be willing to adapt and innovate. Love the Lord deeply. Do the best you can for the Lord not necessarily your superiors."

At age twenty-six, Gifty officially became an osofomaame, and has since embraced her role and serves as a support to her husband. She is a career woman, now forty-seven. Sundays are her busiest as she has other meetings to attend after church service. The Church of Pentecost Osofomaame has a bachelor's degree in Basic Education and presently lives in Koforidua. Using herself as an example, she says it is not true that some of her colleagues are selective in associating with members and that fashion is out of the equation.

As a mother to all, her challenge is how to love all equally. To stay relevant, she recommends the need to love all equally. She admonishes others to always pray for lost souls to be won.

Thirty-eight years old Pat, has a Master's degree and an Osofomaame of The Church of Pentecost. She is now nine years into it, and supports her husband by organizing the women's and children's ministries, counseling, and also in charge of managing the home. Combining ministry, family life and other responsibilities are her challenges. As a career wife, she cannot be specific when it comes to what her busiest day is, "but as duty demands, I become busy as we attend meetings." She believes that when pastors' wives with children under age ten are given some space to manage the "home ministry," they would be more effective in ministry and advance kingdom business. Pat describes ministry as an honorable call which is involving and needs much attention. She advises young or new entrants to support their husbands in every way and not look at the benefits but the rewards. She argues that as a human institution some wives can be selective in associating with members, adding that even though that is not the case, some people tend to isolate themselves and peddle wrong information that they are rather selective. She said it is false for anyone to think ministry is all about fashion.

From Ghana's capital, Accra, SA is a daughter of ministers of the gospel, who married at age twenty-four to the love of her life. Her desire was to marry a pastor and so was glad when nine years after marriage her dream became a reality. Since then, she has been supporting her husband's ministry and work as much as she can in The Church of Pentecost. The MPhil holder, says it is not true they are selective. "We only give attention to those who really need it at any point in time. Just like our children in the home, when one falls sick, you definitely give that child more attention. That's how it is with our work. However, we love everyone the same way." The thirty-four-year-old career woman says her Saturdays and Sundays are the busiest, because of the many social events as it is their work day as ministers and mostly used for visitation.

Ministry in The Church of Pentecost, SA says, is such that they can hardly create enough time to have quality fellowship with their children. She recommends, the need to be more supportive of their role and to be able to make enough time for their children to train them and support them, to avoid any regrets in the future. She asserts: "Marrying a pastor is an honorable thing but it can be quite challenging in every aspect of life. You need to be courageous and determined in order to be fulfilled. Being all things to all people is one major characteristic of this work. I will encourage you to marry a pastor if only you are ready for such changes in your life."

Hetty is a thirty-eight-year-old bachelor's degree holder in Communications Studies. She is currently stationed in Navrongo, the Upper East Regional capital. She is in her eighth year as an Osofomaame in The Church of Pentecost, a calling she has embraced whole heartedly. Over the eight years of supporting her husband's ministry, she identifies, the underlisted as some challenges associated with her life as a pastor's wife:

a. Not being able to 'enjoy' your husband since you are sharing him with so many people (church members).

b. Your children not being able to attend "proper" schools if you are posted to a place without good schools unless you are willing to leave them with relatives and friends which also comes with its own challenges.

c. Inability to pursue your career due to tight schedules of ministry life and also depending on where you are posted, etc.

On the issue of fashion and dressing, she says it is false. However, touching on the osofomaame's selectivity in associating with church members, she states that it depends on the personality of the individual involved. However, since the question uses the word some, she cannot totally deny it, adding that sometimes it is a perception.

As a career lady, her Saturdays are her busiest "I have to do house chores and still blend them with the many ministry activities I couldn't attend to over the week because of my career. I believe the Lord still has better plans for our lives and our careers are still relevant in the ministry even if you don't get a chance to pursue it fully." She has no regrets entering ministry yet, but advises young ladies who want to marry pastors, that the pastor's wife's life is not about fashion or position but service.

Ju had always wanted to marry a pastor, however that wish happened after two years into marriage. She married at age twenty-eight in The Church of Pentecost to the love of her life without any challenges from her parents. Now, four years in ministry, Ju lives in Accra, where her roles involve prayer, good human relations, training young women to become better, providing counseling, supporting the ministry whichever way and so on.

The B.Sc Commerce holder says her challenges as an Osofomaame include, fear of the unknown, financial, inadequate time in caring for herself, among others. As a career woman, Ju is always busy and so for her, all days are equal. She believes spending more time in the presence of God will help her to become more effective for kingdom advancement.

Being a pastor's wife is an honorable work and it takes ladies who have passion for the things of God and are willing to make sacrifices to succeed. To young ladies, she says, "When the calling comes do not hesitate. Always know that the work is prayer and prayer is the work." Instead of being selective, she advises her colleagues to embrace all members as friends, but be careful who they associate with. She says, it is false for people to think ministry is about fashion and dressing.

A daughter of ministers of the gospel, fifty-year-old, Lady AA is with The Apostolic Church, Ghana. She married at age thirty-two with the blessings of her parents. Currently stationed at Aflao, in the Volta Region of Ghana, she holds a Master's Degree in Educational Leadership and Management and has been in ministry for six years now and has since been helping her husband in his ministry, supporting him at home while protecting his dignity and integrity.

Lady AA mentions lack of quality time with her husband, criticism from church members, the need to always be careful, and financial constraint as her challenges in ministry. The career pastor's wife says, "not everyone can be said to be selective in associating with church members. There are individual differences. For me, I'm not selective at all."

She is busiest on Saturdays, occupied with house chores and attending other special social programs with her husband. She believes that making more time for studying and attending in-service training would make her more effective for advancement in ministry.

Lady AA says, "When a pastor is called, I think that his wife has also been called, so any form of training the pastor goes through should be same for the wife. The pastor should not attend Bible School leaving the wife."

GSB, married at twenty-four, and at twenty-five, became an Osofomaame in The Church of Pentecost, and is now twenty-four years in ministry.

The fifty-two-year-old career wife, has an MPhil in Counselling Psychology, M.Ed. Guidance and Counselling, and B. Ed. Social Sciences. Osofomaame GSB, says, "The Church does not have any constitutional role for the pastor's wife. Our role is relative and assumed. Personally, I pray, teach the word of God, counsel the congregation, provide guidance services, perform domestic chores, and any other thing that can be done to complement my husband's ministry."

GSB, from her residence somewhere in the Central Region of Ghana, cites spiritual impediments and attacks, uncooperative leaders, entitlement mentality of some "Area Heads" and their wives, opposition from Women's Ministry leadership as some of the challenges associated with her role as a pastor's wife. In answering the bit about selectivity, she had this to say, "It depends on the personality of the individual involved. I am very democratic and humane. I treat my members with unconditional positive regard, and it is false for anyone to think ministry is all about fashion and dressing."

Weekdays are her busiest as a career woman, as she has to make it to her secular job alongside church programs. In making suggestions for effective kingdom advancement, she thinks opportunities should be available for the osofomaame to add value to their lives through seminars, Career and Professional Development (CPD), and in-service training. Asafomaame should be given defined roles in the church constitution to prevent role ambiguity. Osofomaame advices her colleagues, especially freshers to trust in the faithfulness of the Almighty God and also depend on the Holy Ghost for directions and guidance. She calls on pastors' wives to understand their husbands' calling and support them accordingly.

From the United Kingdom, forty-three-year-old RA, trained both locally and internationally and currently holds an LLB, LLM MSW. She is from The Church of Pentecost stock. Though she had not always wanted to marry a pastor, ministry came after marriage. Today, she has been serving as a pastor's wife for the past fifteen years, having married at age twenty-four. Touching on her role as a pastor's wife she puts it this way, "Sometimes I feel undefined. On one hand, you are in ministry together with your husband, but on the other hand you're just a woman who may not necessarily be acknowledged in the absence of your husband." As a career woman, she thinks the sacrifices she makes to the detriment of her own well-being and at times those of her children, financial and health challenges are her trials. For RA, fashion is a non-starter and the notion that they are selective in associating with members is not true. She adds, however, that relationship takes two people so "I relate to people as they wish to be related to. You cannot force yourself on people." For her, every day is busy since there is always something happening.

RA believes a balanced ministry and family life, devoid of resentment and guilt and time to look after her children, will make her more effective in ministry for kingdom advancement. She has no regrets being in ministry. She calls on new entrants to just be open-minded and take it a day at a time. "Do not have unrealistic expectations as it is a life of work and service." She advises them to depend on God who calls, for He is faithful and also be true to themselves and their identity. She adds they should not kowtow to others' unrealistic expectations of them for it will be too much hard work.

Fifty-year-old SK has a degree and lives in London. he married at twenty-four and has been in it for the past twenty-six years and is in her twentieth year as a pastor's wife. The call to ministry came two years after marriage. During these twenty years, she has been assisting her husband in ministry through her giftings. She is always pressed for time as she combines ministry life with secular life, being a mother and a wife. SK does not agree with the assertion that ministry for asafomaame has been reduced to dressing or fashion. The career mother, says Saturdays are her busiest. Even though she has no regrets being in ministry, her challenge however has to do with "daily offering oneself as a living sacrifice unto God."

From the port city of Tema in the Greater Accra Region of Ghana, comes forty-two-year-old GA, who married at twenty-eight. She is a tertiary school graduate radio journalist and an Asafomaame of the Assemblies of God, Ghana. Currently in her thirteenth year in ministry, over the period she has served and continues to oversee and operate in the Children's Ministry. She is a mentor to young singles and Missionette. For this reason, she leads an exemplary lifestyle and acts as an Advisor to the Women's Ministry. GA says, even though "the role of the pastor's wife is not stated in black and white in her church, the position places a lot of pressure on the Osofomaame. The need to please members and know it all can be a burden. The expectation to be perfect can be a great challenge." She says, false is the assertion that ministry for the pastor's wife is all about dressing and fashion, and that there is nothing like being selective in dealing with members, but rather being careful in relating more with those who are welcoming and warm up to me." Personally, she tries to be friendly to all. As a career mother all the days are busy days. She works six days, a week in a shift system that runs even on weekends. She also holds leadership positions that keep her busy all the time. Any window of opportunity available for her not to work full time as osofomaame would help her to become more effective for kingdom advancement.

"Being a pastor's wife comes with a lot of responsibility. It is a difficult task and young ladies must be prepared as they become the pillar and number one supporter of the pastor."

You have had a peek into the lives of these asafomaame and how they are coping, now is time to acquaint yourself with their struggles or challenges.

CHALLENGES SOME PASTORS' WIVES FACE

Reading through the views shared by our pastors' wives, reveals mixed feelings, and it comes out strongly that ministry like any other endeavor comes with some forms of challenges, no matter the denomination and location of the Osofomaame, be it home or abroad. Let's look at a few of them.

Most definitely, some of our Asofomaame are concerned about some church members' high expectation of them. The members forget that the Word of God says, no one is perfect or righteous. Strangely, they forget that, the Osofomaame is equally human like themselves, and expect them to live above reproach. The least offence and they find it difficult to forgive them. How do we expect to be forgiven when we offend our friends and cannot forgive Osofomaame when she errs? Clearly, this is extra burden for the already stressed pastor's wife. The call is for church members to forgive them as they also forgive. Asafomaame on the other hand should know that "leadership" comes with challenges.

Following on the heels of the high expectation of members of the Osofomaame is also the unrealistic demand from some church members. For some members, the Osofomaame should always be a provider when it comes to support, especially financially. Seeing the Osofomaame modestly and decently dressed, portrays all is well with her and once she is unable to meet their demands then she is not a "proper Osofomaame" or not Christlike. This situation comes about because some members think the pastor and his wife are well paid, hence financially stable. This unrealistic demand by some members which is a source of concern for the asafomaame ought to be understood. Working for the owner of the whole universe who has the whole world in His hands means that asafomaame should be financially sound so as to support members. It, therefore, means that asafomaame should have some form of sustainable income.

As a result of their undefined roles, the situation sometimes leads to clashes between the Women's Ministry leaders and the Osofomaame, where each thinks the other is assuming their roles. This is where the call for streamlining the roles of the Osofomaame comes in. Once this is put in black and white it will reduce the friction. The women's leaders and asafomaame should learn to work hand in hand and not create any unpleasant conditions for young believers.

There is also a perception out there that all the offerings of the church end up in the mission house and the pastor and his family use it at their pleasure. This is a huge challenge for some safomaame. Why would some members even think this way? This is because, they may not be privy to how such offerings are used. To correct this perception, leadership can use their platforms to once in a while explain to church members the disbursement of church funds. Asafomaame who feel bad about this perception should also ensure they use the least opportunity to educate members on this issue.

For some career Asafomaame, their inability to balance work with ministry life weighs them down. Striking a balance is nearly impossible because they cannot select attending some church programs over others and they end up stressed up. One may also want to know how other career deaconesses go about their work and still do church work. Maybe, these Asafomaame can learn from them. The truth is that, it is possible to strike a balance if they plan their lives well. The word of God says, there is time for everything. With proper planning devoid of the desire to please leadership, osofomaame should be able to balance their lives. Again, by some unwritten code, the Osafomaame is expected to be at all church programs with the pastor not just for attending sake but also to avoid any form of temptations. How does the career woman get to operate or practice her profession fully with all such packed programs? The answer is simply effective planning.

In spite of all the support asafomaame give to their husbands in ministry, some say their work is not even quantified, let alone paid for by the church. This, indeed is a headache for some. If they leave everything to work hand in hand with pastor, why not give them some form of stipend? The laborer deserves his wages, says the Bible, and this must be looked into. If they are also supposed to support members and their families, some form of remuneration no matter how small will give them the edge to meet some of such requests from members and family.

A major challenge for a high percentage of Asafomaame borders on transfers, which lead to disruption of family life, especially that of their children, affecting their education. When they are transferred from one location to another, especially to areas where educational institutions are not up to standard, they are unable to go on transfer with their children. In such situations, they have no choice but to leave their children with family and friends which also comes with its own challenges. Since education is the bedrock of all societies, leadership can put in place strategies to help solve this disruption in education of pastors' children during transfers.

Is it not strange that the Osofomaame who serves as a counselor and advisor to the church public has no one to turn to, when she sometimes needs same advice? This is indeed a concern for some. It will give them some relief if a compulsory system for counseling could be put in place, so that the pastor and his wife can go there for professional counseling every quarter.

As the pastor serves as the father for the church, hardly does Osofomaame get to enjoy her husband or marriage life. Pastor is always on the go; he leaves home early and gets back late. Quality family time is almost impossible and this affects Asafomaame as they feel lonely. Even on Mondays which is supposed to be their Sabbath, they are still attending to some church members. Can pastors also help themselves be heeding the advice Jethro gave to Moses? Can they prioritize the concerns of members by allowing some elders to help them?

Some Area Heads are said to be uncooperative and feel so entitled to the extent that working with the pastor is a challenge not to even talk of the Osofomaame. There is no where in the Bible Jesus Christ and his disciples struggled over roles. Can Area Heads delegate and give pastors free hands just for the advancement of the Kingdom? Let them not forget members watch closely. If this becomes obvious, it may affect the faith of some. Amicable solutions should be found to such challenges. The leader, in this case the Area Head, should learn to lead.

The health of some asafomaame has been affected in the cause of the discharge of their duties, leading to permanent health conditions, yet they are soldiering on. Same way some encounter spiritual attacks in the discharge of their unscripted roles as they advance the kingdom of God side by side their husbands - pastors. The Bible never promised a problem feel assignment. Jesus, however, promises to go through the struggles with us, in this case, them. The advice is for them to go labor on.

How do pastors get trained and their partners (asofomaame) do not get trained? This situation, they wish, will be given a second thought, as equal or some form of training will do them good for all. Lack of training for them is a springboard for some form of disrespect and dysfunctional relations. A critical look should be taken at this to make Asafomaame more effective. The good news, however, is that The Church of Pentecost now has a structured form of training for all ministers' wives which some have started attending. In denominations where such systems are not available, leadership can take a cue from them.

After all the work they do, Asafomaame do not get any financial reward for all their contribution to the kingdom business. Some form of remuneration will help them also do good to others, as financial challenges are giving them "bad press."

Indeed, the Osofomaame encounters challenges, yet not a single one out of the thirty-five respondents regrets being in ministry, as they know their labor will not be in vain. The truth is that even the master Jesus Christ went through challenges and overcame them for the higher crown. I wish to encourage our church mothers not to give up, but to continue to look up to Jesus, the author and finisher of their faith, who is busily preparing a place for the righteous. If this is the case, then their grievances when looked at properly by the powers that be will do both leadership and church members a lot of good.

From giving us a glimpse into some of their struggles, we want to read about their recommendations and suggestions.

RECOMMENDATIONS/ SUGGESTIONS

In spite of all the challenges stated above, the Asafomaame took time to make some suggestions and recommendations for the attention of leadership and young ladies who are considering ministry life.

About ninety percent of respondents are of the view that prayer is key for a successful ministry life. They request that church members understand that they are humans just like them and are also fallible. While calling on leadership to consider instituting a system of giving them some form of allowances or putting them on pay roll to cushion them, they believe periodic workshops and training will help them to improve upon their ministry to face the dynamic world system. Again, they would want to also attend Bible school with their husbands. Above all, they would love for them to be given clear roles as pastors wives to eliminate clashes with some women ministry leaders. Furthermore, those with children below age ten be given some space to take care of them and also allow them enjoy their husbands while career women allowed to practice fully.

Now let's turn our attention to what messages and advice they have for new entrants for ministry.

Ten

MESSAGE FOR NEW ENTRANTS/ YOUNG PASTORS' WIVES

As some pastors' wives age, retire, and naturally die, new and young ladies along with their husbands get called into ministry. The forebears or "seniors" advise the new entrants to know that ministry is a calling and, so, they should prepare themselves spiritually and in all spheres. They should study and live the Bible.

Ladies considering ministry should avoid discrimination, be approachable, build a good relationship with all members, come with a servant's heart and not look forward to being served. Ministry is prayer and prayer is the ministry. In short, the following would help them enjoy ministry:

- They should be willing to adapt and be innovative.

- They should be prayerful and serious with their spiritual life.

- They should be approachable.

- They should be all embracing by having a mother's mindset being a mother to all.

- Above all, they should be prayerful and supportive of their husband's ministry.

All this writing came about due to the sudden demise of a bosom friend, the late Mrs. Hannah-Osei-Korsah. Our friendship started from the Burma Camp Worship Center.   It is, therefore, right that we take views from people who one way or the other knew her. The next chapter, therefore, brings you views from them.

VIEWS FROM BURMA CAMP

Hannah basically grew up in The Church of Pentecost Burma Camp, now the Garrison Church of Pentecost, where she became a Sunday School Teacher before marriage took her away. Here, you will read from some church members who were either her fellow Sunday school teachers, members, her own Sunday school pupils, elders, deacons and deaconesses. As at the time of writing, some had become church leaders, pastors and Asofomaame. Take a read about what they have to say about our dear late friend, sister and Osofomaame.

"I know Hannah to be a soft-spoken person, always with smiles. She was very humble and honest."
Pastor Kwasi Adomako

"She was a lovely Sunday school teacher."
Mrs. Ruby Mankatta

"Hannah was a down-to-earth person, who wouldn't hurt a fly. She was affable, ready to listen to anything you bring before her."
Deacon Wisdom Anyakpah

"She was assertive, frank and a prayer warrior."
Osofomame Fidelia Akua Nyarko Sarfo

"She was humble, God-fearing, principled and relied on God. This made her achieve many goals set before her."
Deaconess Philomina Osei

"Sister Hannah was a good sister to me. She and I served as ushers and counselors in the La Area. The last program we attended was at the Trade Fair site, chaired by Chairman Martinson Kwadwo Yeboah. We taught Sunday school together."
Teacher Adu Atta

"Hannah feared God and loved Jesus. She loved the things of God and was a woman of prayer. I will forever remember her. May her soul rest in peace."
Pastor George Ayisi Asare

"She was obedient, sober, respectful, a hard worker, woman of integrity, prayerful, and adviser."
Elder Samuel Amoah

"Osofomaame Hannah was someone who had respect for human beings, young and old. She did not talk harsh or shout on top of her voice to her peers whenever there is an argument or misunderstanding. She did not say 'yes' easily or get annoyed easily like me, but always showed her teeth. But if she got annoyed then stand well. She did not know gossip as some ladies do. If you tried to talk about someone she would say, "I will tell or

ask him or her." She always tried to do the right thing anytime anywhere. Let me pause."
Elder John Amelemah

"HANNAH was a very dedicated and committed Christian, very respectful, a hard-working personality, very disciplined, very dependable. She was a very strong-willed woman (she knew what she wanted and would go for it). She was quick to accept her fault and apologize when she made a mistake or went wrong. She was very serious with her work. She was always wanted to learn. She was very friendly and always smiling."
Elder Enoch Larbi

"Growing up, sister Hannah and I were Sunday school mates. Upon graduating to the adult church service, we became very close friends. We made time to go and pray at a school park, what we termed "park so" literally. She was my role model, and I learnt a lot from her. She taught me to be prayerful, perseverance, and to speak up when need be. She will always have a place in my heart. Love."
Teacher Happy Teye

Twelve

TRIBUTES

Mrs. Hannah Osei-Korsah was finally laid to rest on Saturday, November 19, 2022 in the Ghanaian national capital, Accra. Before that, a memorial service was held for her at the Taifa District at Achimota Central Assembly, her last Area before her untimely death. I share with you tributes as were read by the various persons and groups. This will give you an inkling of the person I am struggling to forget.

TRIBUTE BY WIDOWER

"My wife is now described as a 'body'?" I exclaimed; fresh tears coursing down my checks. Driving at top speed to the hospital and praying simultaneously on that fateful day, the fear of losing her, hung on my mind.

Our first meeting was at KNUST as a Central Committee (CC) member, planning for a National PENSA conference after which she was officially recommended to me. I remember that during Apostle Ayerakwas's welcome service to New Tafo, just seeing her was more important than anything going on. How can I forget the shirt I wore that fateful day when I proposed to her made my work easier? It had the inscription BMW which I translated as "Be My Wife" when I showed it to her. How can I forget standing still in the phone booth for hours, waiting for her call when it was raining cat and dogs? The top speed with which I run to receive my letter from the pigeonhole at Porter's Lodge knowing it was from her. Not forgetting portion of songs of Solomon captured in correspondence we frequently had.

A woman I loved and cherished so much. My roommate and partner understood me and put all my needs above all. I never left home hungry, no matter how late I was. She made sure I looked good and always complimented me. Our love was so pure that we understood each other so well and knew who must keep quiet when an exchange erupted.

A virtuous lady, a Christian mother, a loving wife and a great counsellor – A counsellor to the counselor. She has been the fuel that drove me to excel in this ministry. Her beauty was astounding and I could not bear to express it publicly. The intimacy we shared proved to me that she was indeed from out of my ribs, our wedding day was on 31st October 2000 when I put the ring on her finger as a token of my love. She chose to leave on a memorable day, the date we tied the knot. It was exactly 22 years on October 31st 2022, when I was asked to take the ring from her finger when she was being prepared to be sent to the cold room.

Who will help me sing the songs I raise before and during sermons? A real home manageress who always planned and stocked her home with necessary items well before time. She barely left basic items when we were traveling due to her nature of planning ahead which I greatly contrast.

Death has laid it icy hands on beloved Hannah. I will miss everything about her. Her joy on the eve of her departure gives me a great insight into the joy she is feeling right now in heaven. I loved and cherished her, but God loves her best. It is very difficult to release what one loves; but it becomes less difficult when what one loves is released into the hands of the Almighty. We are mere travelers on earth, heaven is our home; that is the summary of our ministry. If she has gotten there, then I am happy for her.

May my love rest in perfect peace.

TRIBUTE BY CHILDREN

People, so great and small, dignitaries we meet once in a blue moon, gracing this occasion. We stand before this lectern and allow our eyes to feed on this gathering and are indeed intrigued by the numbers so huge. Then we ask ourselves; "is there not a cause?" This is not to celebrate another farewell service or any of our weddings but to celebrate a great woman who once lived. Our own dear mother.

Beloved, a hardworking golden heart has stopped beating; hardworking hands are at rest. God has affirmed that He only takes the best due to her exemplary lifestyle. As a Christian, mummy was true to her faith and she always taught us to always acknowledge the presence of the Holy Spirit in our lives and also keep God first in whatever we do. She was a teacher of the Word and very practical in delivering her sermons to the admiration of all. She was very passionate when it comes to worship and leading songs of the cross during communion service. She was daddy's melodious voice. Mummy loved dancing and even danced during the special evening service with the Chairman on the eve of her departure. She was a very prayerful woman and she taught us to always talk to God. Whenever we approached mummy with our problems, she would ask us if we had already spoken to Jesus about them. We admired how she supported daddy in the ministry; making it a point to be present at every church programme. Her ability to combine ministerial duties with her work as a headmistress deserves to be applauded.

Mama was a perfectionist; she ensured that everything was done well. There were times she woke us from sleep when we did not effectively do our chores because she believed and always said; "if it must be done, it must be done well." Mummy was our friend, sister, counselor, teacher, and a disciplinarian. She used to tell us that "M'anwo wo sɛ me bɛyɛn wo." Nokware w'anyɛn yɛn na mmom w'atete yɛn Nyame suro ne abrabɔ pa mu," and for that we are grateful.

Mummy was so hospitable and generous. She was a friend and a mother to all. Always willing to listen to us and offer help. Her arms and doors were open to all at any time of the day and no visitors ever left empty-handed. Her smiles were so overwhelming and so particular about the welfare of others. We learned the importance of hospitality from this great woman.

Mummy always looked flamboyant whenever she stepped out and even at home. She always knew how to dress to suit the occasion. With very few accessories, she stood out. Stella, Florence, and Phyllis were her fashion consultants. They always filled her room to help her choose an outfit for church. She loved taking pictures; she always took pictures after church service and she had so many pictures which several copies of this brochure cannot contain.

When it comes to home management, mummy executed her duties very well. We never lacked anything. Mummy made sure she gave us everything we needed and even more. She always wanted us around her when preparing a meal. In the kitchen, we all had a role to play; Emmanuel was her inventory manager, Ebenezer was her personal assistant, and Stella, Florence and Phyllis took turns in preparing dishes keenly supervised by her.

Who will shout our names like she used to? Who will call us to help select her outfit for service on Sundays? Who will constantly call to check up on us in school? We have a grudge against death because it has laid its icy hands on our treasured possession. It is painful but we are not hopeless. We do not cry like those of the world because we know the best thing has happened to her. We know she is resting in the Lord's bosom, reuniting with her mum and dad. We know she is happy where she is and that is our hope and joy.

Till we meet again

Nyame mfa no nsie, Mama Ama Nyamaa Obataan pa.

May her precious soul rest in perfect peace.

TRIBUTE BY GHANA EDUCATION SERVICE – NZEMA EAST MUNICIPAL EDUCATION DIRECTORATE, AXIM

"We do not live for ourselves only, and we do not die for ourselves only. If we live, it's for the Lord that we live, and if we die, it is for the Lord that we die. So, whether we live or die, we belong to the Lord." – Romans 14:7-8

"Some people come into our lives and quickly go. Some stay for a while, leave footprints our hearts, and we are never, ever the same." – Flavia Weedn

We are profoundly saddened as we are gathered here today.

EDUCATION OFFICE

To all and sundry who got acquainted with Mrs. Hannah Osei-Korsah, the headteacher of Apewosika MA Basic School, Axim, demystified the saying that "Life is very fleeting" but brings in fond memories when it is well-lived.

Mrs. Hannah Osei-Korsah was a professionally trained teacher with the rank of Assistant Director II. She joined Ghana Education Service on the 1st of September 1998. She was re-posted from New Abossey Okai Basic School (Laterbiokorshie, Accra) to Nzema East Municipal Education Service, Axim on the 1st of September 2018 as a class teacher to teach English at Apewosika M/A Basic, in Axim South Circuit. However, two months after her posting, Mrs. Hannah Osei-Korsah was appointed as the headteacher of the school on 15th October 2018 due to the transfer of the then headteacher. She was present at all general meetings and contributed her ideas when necessary.

APEWOSIKA M/A BASIC SCHOOL

Mrs. Hannah Osei-Korsah took the mantle of leadership and ran with it. she was a disciplined leader who served as an exemplary role model for both teachers and students.

Madam Hannah had a course to take a tough decision and her greatness and success lay in the fact that she was both tough-minded and tender-hearted.

She worked hard as a headmistress to raise the profile of the school and it is now like a city on the hill. Madam Hannah always made sure that rules and regulations were adhered to by teachers, students, and even parents. Her presence at every official gathering was inspiring and she would seize the opportunity to talk to her pupils referring to them as "me mba." Not for once did she bend the rules to favour anyone and her passion for the work made her always say, "Abban Edwuma Yɛn, soa na Yɛtwe no ase," as well as her two principles in life, "If it must be done, it must be done well" and "Whatever you do, work at it with all your heart, as working for the Lord, not for men" (Colossians 3:23)

Madam Hannah was a woman of results and she proved it. she inspired us the teachers as well as the learners. The school occupied the third and second positions in the 6th March parade in 2019 and 2020, respectively.

It was during her time that the school won the second and first positions in the inter-school Science and Math Quiz and project exhibition in 2019 and 2020, respectively. It was not only academics that she was keen on improving but other co-curricular activities. The school took the first position in the

Drama and Culture Dance at the inter-schools' cultural festival competition in 2020.

She always said, "Yɛde Nkran bɛba Axim" and, indeed, she made it happen. She organised the first ever speech and prize-giving day as well as the career day in the history of the school. Through her hard work and able support of her husband, Apostle Philip Osei-Korsah, she was able to secure an ultra-modern toilet facility for the school from The Church of Pentecost, Axim Area. Her tenure brought the school to the limelight in the area of academic and infrastructure. We are now, if not the best, one of the best public schools in the municipality. How can we speak about her achievements without mentioning that it was during her reign that the school had an aggregate of nine? Hmmm, we remember that day, she could not hide her joy. She said, "it has paid off". We asked her how? She answered, "when I took over, the enrollment of the school was 317 pupils. Now the enrollment has risen to 407". Many National service and NABCO personnel were brought to the school to render their services. Conference of Head of Basic Schools (CoHBS) Madam Hannah was one of the vibrant members of our great association, the conference of Head of Basic School (CoHBS), Nzema East Municipality-Axim.

Her active membership has impacted our noble association with her excellent advice, valuable contributions, and perspectives on any issue that confronted us.

We remember when we first met Madam during one of our meetings, we felt like she was someone we had known, for a much longer time than the four years she had spent with us.

Following her charisma, whenever she spoke, she was listened with rapt attention, not only for what she said but also for the way she said it quietly with decorum, immense authority, and wisdom. Such traits made her endear herself to many.

Although she faced some challenges in the administration of her duties and responsibilities, with prayers, courage, enthusiasm, innovations, and interventions, she fought till the last to improve and excel in the school's records in the Basic Education Certificate Examinations (BECE), coveted positions in sporting activities, March pass, Maths/Science Quizzes, and Cultural Competitions, in the Nzema East Municipality-Axim.

On that fateful Monday morning of 31st October, 2022, teachers were whispering to one another. Everyone's facial expression suddenly became pale and sorrowful.

What is happening? What has happened? Only to be told of her death.

Hmmm! Today is particularly a difficult and painful time for her family and the school. In extending to them our heartfelt condolences, we wish them the courage and the strength to bear this irreparable loss.

Indeed, death has taken away a genuinely warm individual, a loving wife, mother, sister, and headteacher, and deprived so many others, including us, of a good friend and colleague.

In our sight, Madam Hannah is gone but she remains in our hearts! We never thought we could live and miss someone so much that we feel so empty. Her demise has left a vacuum in all her staff and Apewosika community.

May Madam Hannah rest in celestial peace…

Till we meet again. We wish her Godspeed!

Agɔnwolɛ nee adiema kpalɛ,

Tia boɛ

Nana Nyamenle ɛva wɔ ɛk3la ɛzie boɛ

TRIBUTE BY TAIFA CENTRAL ASSEMBLY

"And I heard a voice from heaven saying, write this: Blessed are the dead who die in the Lord from now on. Blessed indeed, says the Spirit, that they may rest from their labors, for their deeds follow them!"
– Revelations 14:13 (ESV)

Beloved, we are gathered here to bid farewell to our beloved mother, Mrs. Hannah Osei-Korsah, who the Lord has called to join the Church triumphant. We were elated when a circular letter from our Chairman's office announced that Apostle Philip Osei-Korsah and family would now worship with Taifa Central Assembly due to apostle's new appointment as Director of the Counselling Ministry.

When our late mother first attended service with her family, we immediately recognised her as a visionary, graceful, hospitable, inspirational, serene, and unique woman of God. These traits or qualities became the topic of discussion after church service that day. The late Mrs. Hannah Osei-Korsah stayed with us for barely two months and she was seen as the humblest of all. In fact, she was humility personified. Her presence among us epitomised a more servant-like nature.

She would never pass by without smiling and always ensure that those around her were happy. There was never a dull moment with her either at church or home. She always danced during church services. In fact, we recall how she danced enthusiastically even the day before she was called to glory. She was an astute woman, affable and very spiritual. She was the embodiment of wisdom and knowledge.

Maa Hannah was hardworking. This was vividly depicted by how she frequently travelled from Axim to Accra on weekends to check on her family's well-being and attend church on Sundays.

We now comprehend why in Apostle's Korsah message to the assembly on the 30th of the October 2022 during a gospel Sunday Service, he made us reason into the topic, "The Rapture." In his sermon, he prompted us to repent of our transgressions and renew our commitment to God. He discussed the need for a renewal of our minds and hearts as well.

After the sermon by the Apostle, we experienced a kind of bliss we had never encountered. The Church of Pentecost has lost a gem and we will forever keep the memory of her fondly in our hearts till we all congregate again in heaven. We love her, but we accept the decision of Lord Almighty, who loves her most.

May heaven preserve her beloved soul…

Till we meet again

May the Lord keep her in perfect peace.

TRIBUTE BY GENERAL COUNCIL TRIBUTE IN HONOUR OF MRS. HANNAH OSEI-KORSAH

We are gathered here today to mourn our dear mother, wife, sister, colleague and friend whose sudden demise has left her loved ones in total shock. A great woman who made the world a better place just with her cheerful smile; one who was still in the prime of her life, is abruptly gone.

Admittedly, news of her passing brought about a helpless sense of loss, a feeling of disappointment, and many unanswered questions. But on a day like this, we can take solace in the unchanging word of God in Isaiah 57:1-2: "the righteous pass away; the godly often die before their time. No one seems to understand that God is protecting them from evil to come. For those who follow godly paths will rest in peace when they die."

Until her passing, Mrs. Hannah Osei-Korsah, the late wife of our colleague, Apostle Philip Osei-Korsah, proved to be a very hardworking and dedicated minister's wife. She played an instrumental role in the last two decades that the couple served in the full-time ministry of The Church of Pentecost.

Although a professionally trained teacher, she readily adapted to any situation brought about by her husband's ministerial transfers, despite the toll it had on her professional life, and never hesitated to request a transfer from her employers to join her husband at his assigned duty stations. She followed him wherever he went from Jamasi, where they were first stationed, to Tamale, Accra, Axim, and back to Accra.

Such devotion to the heavenly call is worthy of commendation, and all ministers here gathered can attest to the importance of a spouse's unwavering support in the work of the ministry. As a result, the couple was almost inseparable, as they forged a formidable partnership in ministry.

Among other exemplary traits, we also saw her as being god-fearing, respectful, humble, firm and very instructive. Her infectious smiles and great counselling ability were added advantage to her husband's ministry.

Undoubtedly, The Church of Pentecost has lost a virtuous woman who has made a mark in ministry, even in a relatively short period.

The General Council of The Church of Pentecost wishes to express our sincere condolence to the widower, the children, the bereaved families and the entire membership of the Taifa District for this painful loss.

We are confident that Hannah has served the Lord's purpose in her generation and is now resting in peace, as Prophet Isaiah has assured us.

May her soul rest in perfect peace.

Thirteen
CONCLUSION

In this book, an effort has been made to understand who a pastor's wife is, her role in ministry, challenges and the recommendations and suggestions for leadership of various denominations to make them more effective in the advancement of kingdom business.

The need to write this book is based on the untimely death of my dear sister, friend and Osofo maame Mrs. Hannah Osei-Korsah, which has left me with more questions than answers. How would AMA have answered the questioned posed if she were alive? Would she be among those who said they are busy all week round and needed some time for themselves? Would God Almighty explain to us when we meet Him? I cannot tell, accepting the fact that she is no more is a challenge I would have to deal with this for many years more to come. Views from all thirty -three pastors' wives' point to one thing, that there is no clear-cut role put in place for any of them. They, however, support their husbands (pastors) based on their own background and spiritual giftings. This undefined role makes some of them assume certain roles which are supposed to be the preserve of women leaders of the church.

It comes out clearly, that even though, pastors' wives are humans like all others, majority of church members hold them in high esteem just as their pastor husbands and expect them to live above reproach and be all- embracing, something that is not realistic. Nowhere did any of the thirty-four women write about regrets in accepting ministry life. It is however clear that, they get overwhelmed by this and sometimes work load, weighing them down especially, on career women who have to joggle between ministry and regular work schedules. They are of the view, that when measures are put in place and streamlined, it would put them in a better position to serve their families well, balance ministry with their personal life, reduce stress and above all contribute effectively to kingdom advancement.

The combination of roles by the career Osofomaame is where my dear late Mrs Hannah Osei-Korsah comes in, as some of the respondents agree that they become so busy that they barely have any life of their own. Can our mothers slow down, and rest once in a while? Could they retreat, take a rest and continue rather than wanting to be at all programs to please people? Could they also pay attention to their health needs? the questions are many, we will however understand it better one day.

Let me place on record, that all who took part in this project are educated women, the youngest being thirty-one years and the oldest fifty-five. The least of the educational background is a BECE, which is the basic certificate, with the highest being a medical doctor. This therefore means, that the thirty-five respondents know exactly what they are doing and what they consider necessary for their effectiveness and advancement.

It is clear, that the life of the pastor's wife can be described as a case of "buy one, get one free," in the sense that, even though, it is their husbands who are officially called into ministry, they become the bonus "free commodity"- the individual who is supposed to add unto ministry to complete their husband's calling. I believe strongly that these mothers of the church have touched on one or two issues, begging the attention of leadership of the various denominations, which when, fine-tuned will improve the working life for the spouses. Considering all the challenges and sacrifices the pastor's wives make, would the call to consider some form of remuneration for them, be in the right direction? Time will tell. Until then, adieu my dear sister and friend Mrs. Hannah Osei-Korsah nee Hannah Hammond.

CITED WORKS

Emmanuel A Gyan, (2022), Biography of the late Mrs. Hannah Osei-Korsah Pentecost Press

Frimpong -Manso, Gladys, (2020), The Ideal Minister's Wife, Assemblies of God, Ghana

Kevin G Smith, The Role of the Pastor's Wife: What does the bible Teach? Electronic edition accessed online 4/8/23

Memorial and burial brochure, (2022), Mrs. Hannah Osie-Korsah, Pentecost Press

The Church of Pentecost, Ministerial Handbook, pg. 16&17, (2016), Pentecost Press

Appendix i
GRAPHIC REPRESENTATION OF RESPONSES

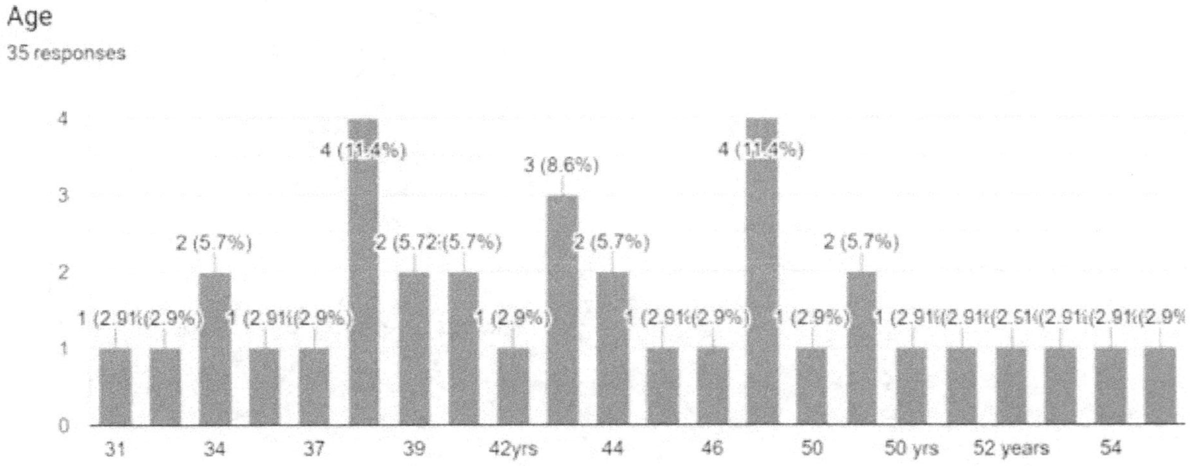

Age

35 responses

Are your parents ministers of the gospel too?

35 responses

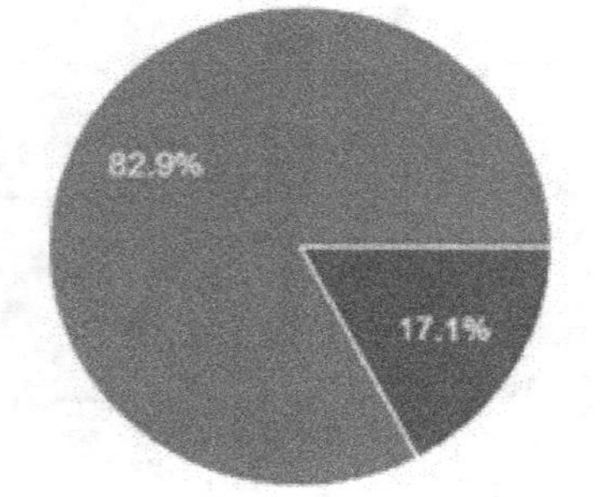

Did your parents oppose to you marrying a Pastor initially?

35 responses

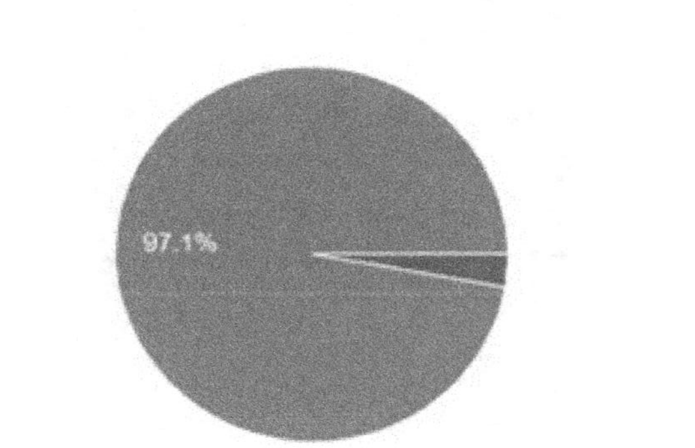

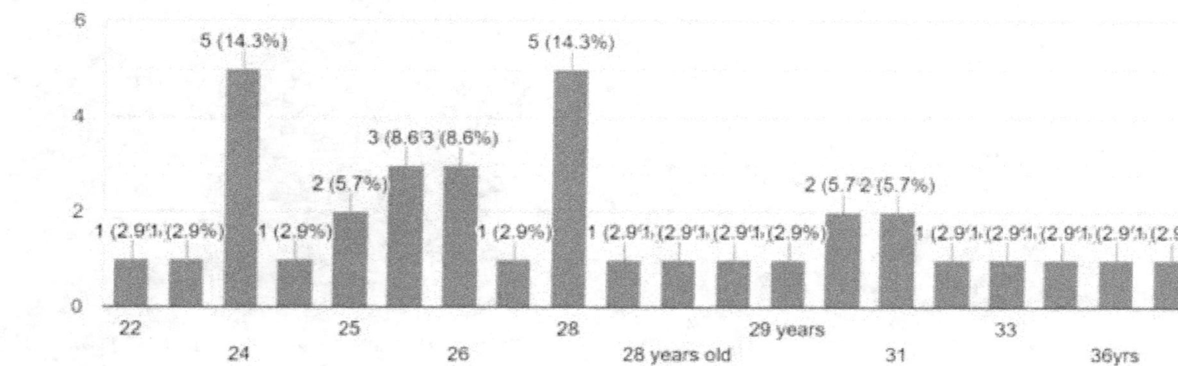

At what age did you marry?
35 responses
6
4
2
0
5 (14.3%)
5 (14.3%)
3 (8.6 3 (8.6%)
2 (5.7%)
2 (5.7 2 (5.7%)
1 (2.9% 1 (2.9%)
1 (2.9%)
1 (2.9%)
1 (2.9% 1 (2.9% 1 (2.9% 1 (2.9%)
1 (2.9% 1 (2.9% 1 (2.9% 1 (2.9% 1 (2.9%
22
24
25
26
28
28 years old
29 years
31
33
36yrs

Did your parents oppose to you marrying a Pastor initially?

35 responses

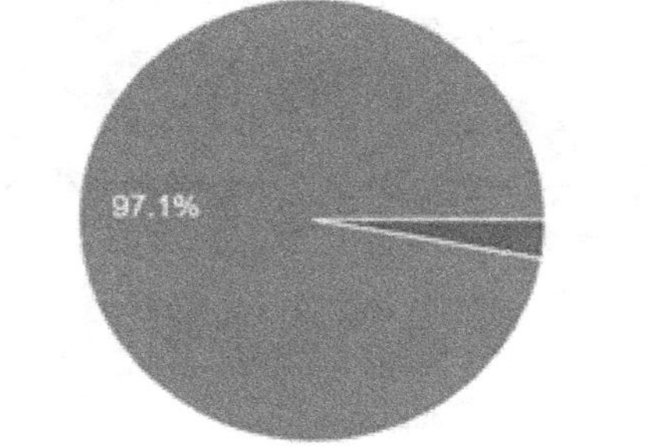

Did you marry a Pastor from scratch, or it was after marriage that he became a Pastor?

35 responses

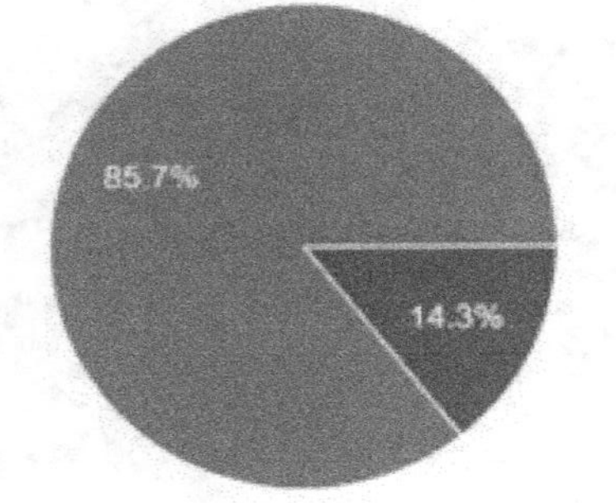

Have you always wanted to be a Pastor's wife?

35 responses

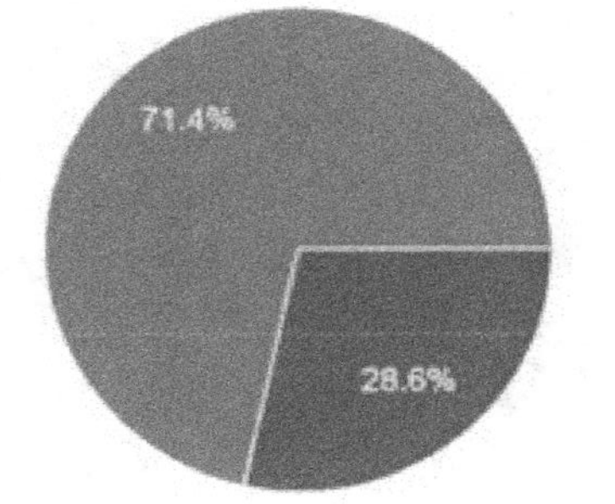

How long have you been a Pastor's wife?
35 responses

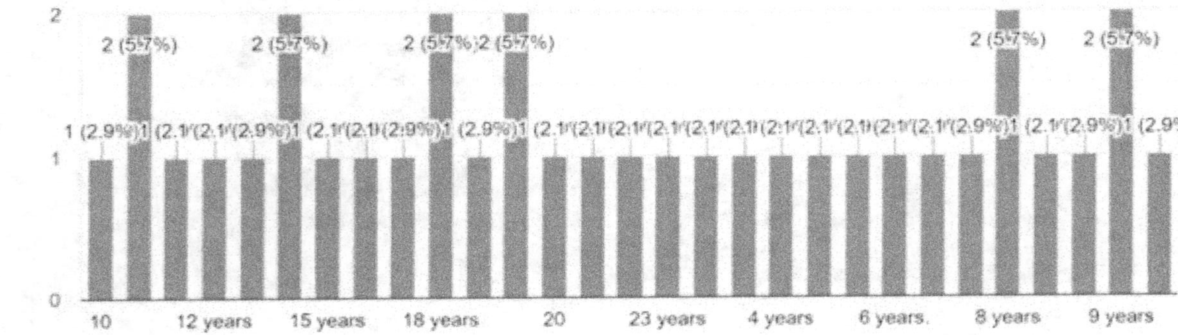

Some say, it is all about fashion/dressing, how true is this?

35 responses

Some think some of you are selective when it comes to associating with members, how true is this?

35 responses

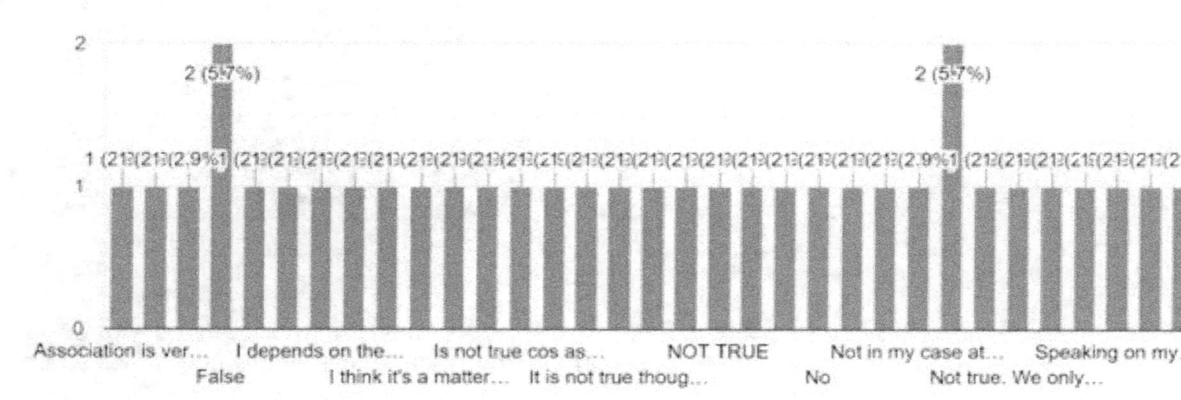

114

Are you a career wife aside being a Pastor's wife or you are a full time Pastor's wife?

35 responses